ALANA VALENTINE's most recent award nomination is the Nick Enright Prize for Drama (NSW Premier's Literary Awards, 2017) for *Ladies Day*. She is the recipient of two Errols (Tasmanian Theatre Awards, 2017) for *The Tree Widows*, which was awarded Best Writing (Professional Production) and the overall Judges' Award for her 'creative integration of community, culture and heritage'. Alana was also nominated for an Errol for Best Director (Professional Production) for *The Tree Widows*. In 2017 Alana is again working with Bangarra Dance Theatre as dramaturg on *Bennelong*, after successful collaborations on their productions *Patyegarang* and *ID*. *Barbara and the Camp Dogs*, co-written with Ursula Yovich, will be produced by Belvoir in December 2017. In November 2017, Venus Theatre Company (USA) will world premiere Alana's play *The Ravens*. An extensive national tour of *Letters to Lindy* is planned for 2018. Alana's website is www.alanavalentine.com.

Jeanette Cronin as Lindy Chamberlain in Merrigong Theatre Company's 2016 production. (Photo: Lisa Tomasetti)

LETTERS TO LINDY
ALANA VALENTINE

Currency Press, Sydney

CURRENCY PLAYS

First published in 2017
by Currency Press Pty Ltd,
PO Box 2287, Strawberry Hills, NSW, 2012, Australia
enquiries@currency.com.au
www.currency.com.au

Copyright: Foreword © Lindy Chamberlain-Creighton, 2016; Introduction © Bryce Hallett, 2017; *Letters to Lindy* © Alana Valentine, 2016, 2017.

COPYING FOR EDUCATIONAL PURPOSES

The Australian *Copyright Act 1968* (Act) allows a maximum of one chapter or 10% of this book, whichever is the greater, to be copied by any educational institution for its educational purposes provided that that educational institution (or the body that administers it) has given a remuneration notice to Copyright Agency Limited (CAL) under the Act.

For details of the CAL licence for educational institutions contact CAL, 11/66 Goulburn Street, Sydney, NSW, 2000; tel: within Australia 1800 066 844 toll free; outside Australia 61 2 9394 7600; fax: 61 2 9394 7601; email: info@copyright.com.au

COPYING FOR OTHER PURPOSES

Except as permitted under the Act, for example a fair dealing for the purposes of study, research, criticism or review, no part of this book may be reproduced, stored in a retrieval system, or transmitted in any form or by any means without prior written permission. All enquiries should be made to the publisher at the address above.

Any performance or public reading of *Letters to Lindy* is forbidden unless a licence has been received from the author or the author's agent. The purchase of this book in no way gives the purchaser the right to perform the play in public, whether by means of a staged production or a reading. All applications for public performance should be addressed to Creative Representation, 206/1 Marian Street Redfern NSW 2016, ph: 02 9690 590; email: sharne@creativerep.com.au

Cataloguing-in-publication data for this title is available from the National Library of Australia website: www.nla.gov.au

Typeset by Dean Nottle for Currency Press.
Cover image by AP / Anonymous.
Image shows Lindy Chamberlain-Creighton.
Cover design by Emma Rose Smith (for Currency Press).
Cover concept by Merrigong Theatre Company.

Foreword

People have been coming to me for the last thirty-five years and saying, 'We really must do something with the letters in the library, they're fascinating'. And so I'd say, 'Yes, you can have a look at them and see what you think'.

Once people started reading the collection of letters they would think, 'Oh, I've got to do this'. But then the size and scale of it would overwhelm them and they'd never get any further. They always came back and went, 'Ugh, that's such a job. Too big for me.'

The last person who requested access was Alana Valentine, and she didn't say 'That's such a job, I can't touch that.' She just kept saying, 'That's so interesting, can I look at more of them?' She did, and then she showed them to me and interviewed me about how they were filed.

I read this play and I went all the way through it and I thought, yeah it's okay but probably not finished yet. And I think I laughed once and I didn't cry at all. Not a thing was changed since that first reading but when I saw it on stage I laughed and cried all the way through it. I think Reagan, who saw it with me, did much the same thing.

I don't know how many of you are aware that there is very little in that play, only one scene I think, which is not actual quotes, either from me or quotes from the letters. The only scene that's an amalgamation is the librarians' scene, which gives you more of a feel for what people still think today.

I think Ms Valentine has done a brilliant job. It is probably the most powerful thing that has been done on my story and the most true to the behind-the-scenes of what I lived through.

This was a slice of my life. It will not impact you as it has me, but it will leave its mark all the same. I hope if nothing else you will reflect on the strength and impact that words carry.

Lindy Chamberlain-Creighton
December 2016

Glenn Hazeldine in Merrigong Theatre Company's 2016 production. (Photo: Lisa Tomasetti)

Contents

Foreword
　Lindy Chamberlain-Creighton　　　　　　　　　　v

Introduction
　Bryce Hallett　　　　　　　　　　　　　　　　ix

LETTERS TO LINDY
　Act One　　　　　　　　　　　　　　　　　　1
　Act Two　　　　　　　　　　　　　　　　　　26

Currency Press acknowledges the Traditional Owners of the Country on which we live and work. We pay our respects to all Aboriginal and Torres Strait Islander Elders, past and present.

  Publication of this title was assisted by the Commonwealth Government through the Australia Council, its arts funding and advisory body.

Jeanette Cronin as Lindy Chamberlain in Merrigong Theatre Company's 2016 production. (Photo: Lisa Tomasetti)

INTRODUCTION

There are three things that have divided this nation ...
Conscription, Whitlam and Lindy Chamberlain.

The words are spoken by an unnamed librarian in Alana Valentine's finely-wrought play *Letters to Lindy* as he stacks some of the 20,000 letters that Lindy Chamberlain received during her ordeal of being tried, incarcerated, then exonerated of killing her baby Azaria.

The words, delivered matter-of-factly towards the end of the play, serve as an historical epitaph to an intimate and epic docu-drama spanning more than 30 years, from Azaria's death near Uluru in 1980 to the 2012 coronial ruling that finally ended the legal saga.

The starting point of Valentine's passionate inquiry came in the form of 199 boxes of correspondence at the National Library of Australia; a staggering archive from which the playwright has constructed an intricate, truthful and deeply human account of a case which captured the public's imagination from the moment Lindy Chamberlain uttered the words, 'A dingo's got my baby'. For here was an apparent murder mystery combining potent myths of the Australian outback, Aboriginal folklore, baffling cult-like 'characters' and elements of Greek tragedy. It was a time when the worst excesses of tabloid sensationalism fuelled an unthinking, sometimes brutal, spectator sport. Australia hadn't seen anything like it.

Letters to Lindy bears witness to good and evil of varying hues as it astutely juxtaposes the private and public. Thousands of Australians were compelled to write to Lindy Chamberlain-Creighton in the wake of baby Azaria's death. Many were compassionate and consoling; others hostile and threatening. Remarkably, Chamberlain-Creighton kept them all; the cards, letters, poems and prayers—even, perversely, a single black bootie with a red ribbon. (Meryl Streep, who portrayed Lindy in the film *Evil Angels*, received a matching bootie from the same anonymous source.) One of the letters hailed Azaria as a herald of the second coming of Christ. There were also death threats.

Having 20,000 letters on hand provided Valentine a fertile resource, but making sense of it all and creating a work for the stage that is lucid, thoughtful and absorbing has enormous challenges. Crucially, it requires the trust of its protagonist, leaps of faith, playfulness and purpose. It is here where the authenticity of private reveries about struggle and sacrifice make *Letters to Lindy* a memorable and precious work.

The play opens in the present with Chamberlain-Creighton sifting through archive boxes with a sure and steady hand, a device enabling a variety of stories to flow and flashbacks to be re-enacted. It is akin to the opening of a cold case and, even though we know how it ends, the directness and hard truths of *Letters to Lindy* feel as though information is being unearthed for the first time.

From the archive, or what Valentine calls 'a community', there emerge telling insights into the attitudes of Australian society, the nature of celebrity, a prevailing sense of judgement versus justice, and the grief of a woman who did not conform to expectation. As memories are stirred of the fateful night at the Uluru campsite when Lindy Chamberlain discovered that a dingo had taken her baby, Valentine fills the stage with figures and voices befitting a Greek chorus; an assemblage of first-hand witnesses and second-guessing armchair critics who salivate at the prospect of Chamberlain's demise. Says a figure in the play: 'You're so bloody hard no tears have ever come out of your eyes.'

The audience hears the voices of admirers, sympathisers and haters—the 'nasty ones' as Chamberlain-Creighton lightly condemns them—the majority of whom are ordinary people with no stake in the case. There are, however, notable exceptions, including the British forensic expert James Cameron and the *Sydney Morning Herald* journalist Malcolm Brown, who reported on the case from the outset and formed a close relationship with the Chamberlains. Indeed, Brown became a voice of reason and reassurance amid the melodrama and lynch-mob hysterics.

FOR MANY YEARS Alana Valentine has proved herself to be a rigourous, open-minded, keenly-observant chronicler of Australian society. In a number of instances, the playwright is not merely a detached observer but a champion of the underdog; of people deemed outsiders or outcasts. As evidenced in her plays *Parramatta Girls*, *Run Rabbit Run* and *Ladies Day*, Valentine has the skills of a journalist, the linguistic flair of a dramatist and the instincts and conviction of a social crusader. There is also a lightness of touch, irony and a quick wit.

Authenticity, directness and truth are the hallmarks of her craft and although she can rightly be described as a proponent of verbatim or documentary theatre, the term is limiting given the way Valentine shapes and exploits first-hand interviews and the wealth of material at her disposal.

Like the prolific and prodigious British playwright David Hare (*Stuff Happens*, *The Permanent Way*, *Via Dolorosa*, *The Power of Yes*, to name a few), Valentine is perhaps best described as a truth-teller of the modern stage. She, too, keenly embraces verbatim storytelling shrewdly mixed with fiction and persuasive argument. The writer may appear to vanish to the edges of the page but her voice is there in the shape and order of things, and the way light is shed amid chaos, darkness and strife.

At the height of her powers, Valentine stirs, agitates, cajoles and makes the audience an active participant in the 'community', which is invariably an environment of conflict, struggle, pain and hope. We are invited to wrestle with our conscience and to look beyond black and white. *Letters to Lindy* has the capacity to tear at belief systems. It is testimony to Alana Valentine's craft that she presses disparate facts and confronting realities into service like a conductor of an orchestra; assuredly drawing out rhythms, colours and moods, judiciously using repetition to amplify themes, and turning up the dramatic heat to make the spectator sit up and take notice when it most counts.

An example of this comes in Act One of *Letters to Lindy* as Valentine explores the impact of language and its power to invest the mundane with mythic power. From the moment Lindy Chamberlain uttered the words 'A dingo's got my baby', it was as if her fate was sealed.

LINDY: I thought of the baby not myself
    I didn't get emotional or hysterical
    because I wasn't thinking of myself
    I was thinking there might still be a chance
    so I give the news as clearly and precisely as I can,
    'A dingo's got my baby'.
    So that they don't have to waste time on
    'What is it? What's happened? What's wrong?'

I just screwed it all up into what's happened
and how and the race to fix it.
Because you're in it
it's happening
and she's gone
and you can't undo it
and you can't unlose her
and you can't for a moment
indulge your feelings
so you yell,
'The dingo's got my baby!'
And that's where it begins.

Letters to Lindy is replete with speeches like these. They are unmistakably Australian, forthright, wry, exasperated. Forcefully and poetically the play peels back layers of distortion, accusation and lies to reveal Chamberlain-Creighton's warmth, stoicism, courage and, moreover, her forgiving nature.

Some of the most moving and harrowing scenes involve Lindy's sons and their attempts to reach out for help when all seems lost. Their desperation and concern for their torn-apart mother is conveyed in a letter they have written to the Prime Minister, Prince Charles and Princess Diana. That they write to such well-known figures on the world stage heightens the feeling that they have nowhere else to turn in a battle where enemies, at least on the face of it, outnumber allies.

5th December 1985.
Avondale College, Cooranbong.
Dear Mr Tuxworth, Mr Hawke, Prince Charles and Princess Diana,
   I can still remember the dingo walking on my chest.
   I loved my bubby Azaria and so did Mommy
   We need Mummy at home so does Kahlia need a mommy Can you make them let my mum come home to me
   From Reagan

The climactic Act One scene amplifies the desolation and loss. Lindy receives a phone call about her son, Reagan, and instinct tells her that the news cannot be good.

GUARD: Chamberlain, you've got a phone call.
LINDY: Me?
GUARD: Yes, you.
LINDY: I knew it had to be bad because you weren't allowed calls. So I knew it had to be bad. My son, Reagan, had been standing watching a neighbour's bonfire when a glass bottle that had been thrown into the fire exploded. The shards of glass cut through the right side of his face, slicing his cornea and right eye.
REAGAN: Mummy.
LINDY: He'd been asking for me since it happened.
REAGAN: Mummy.
LINDY: And Reagan is not a child to ask. He's like me, he hides his feelings, but he doesn't understand why he can't be comforted by his mother. They won't let me go down to Mulawa, they won't let me go down to see him, and if he comes to see me, the taking off and landing of getting on a plane is only going to put more pressure on his damaged eye.
REAGAN: Mummy!
LINDY: That was ... that was really hard. That was ... I went down low that time. Lower than I'd been. Low. The next time the family came to visit, Reagan walked in the gate with an eye patch on, and then at the end of the visit when I went to say goodbye to him, he couldn't be found ...

As in Valentine's drawn-from-life drama *Parramatta Girls*, the personal becomes political. The act of rekindling the past is not simple or straightforward. The benefit of hindsight sees that words and deeds accrue any number of ironies and, in some instances, assume a chilling tone.

Letters to Lindy is a story of sacrifice and human resilience. Tests of endurance cumulate into an unyielding rhythm and dramatic intensity through which shines Lindy's unwavering faith and a value system that refuses to succumb to hate in the face of adversity and injustice.

The significance of Valentine's work lies not only in its exploration of an enthralling chapter in Australian history, but in its humanity. The truthful, witty and moving play is arguably more immediate and insightful than the opera (*Lindy*, 2002) or the film (*Evil Angels*,

1988). It succeeds because of the direct and affecting way it reveals the devastating personal cost and burden of a quintessentially Australian woman who, when you think about it, is no different to a relative, friend or neighbour.

Bryce Hallett
March 2017

Bryce Hallett is a former arts editor and chief theatre critic at the *Sydney Morning Herald*. He is the writer of the musical bio-drama *Freeway—The Chet Baker Journey* and the rock drama *Rolling Thunder Vietnam*.

Letters to Lindy was first produced by Merrigong Theatre Company in association with Canberra Theatre Centre at Illawarra Performing Arts Centre, Wollongong, on 26 July 2016, with the following cast:

LINDY	Jeanette Cronin
ENSEMBLE [FIGURE 3]	Glenn Hazeldine
ENSEMBLE [FIGURE 2]	Phillip Hinton
ENSEMBLE [FIGURE 1]	Jane Phegan

Director, Darren Yap
Designer, James Browne
Lighting Designer, Toby Knyvett
Composers and Sound Designers, Max Lambert and Roger Lock

From left: Phillip Hinton, Jeanette Cronin (kneeling) as Lindy Chamberlain, Glenn Hazeldine and Jane Phegan in Merrigong Theatre Company's 2016 production. (Photo: Lisa Tomasetti)

ACKNOWLEDGEMENTS

Seeking permission to use these letters has been a remarkable journey in itself. Having sent out hundreds of permission requests to addresses which are often more than thirty years old, I have been assisted by those who have generously forwarded the letters on to former occupants, by postal services that have returned the envelopes unopened, and by relatives of letter-writers who are deceased.

I wrote to three different Marilyn Nolans in three different states (thank you to the electoral rolls held at the NLA) to get permission to use her incredibly moving letter about meeting Lindy in the Mount Isa maternity ward. I wrote to Lance and Merle Puckeridge at the Mission to Seafarers in Wollongong. It never reached them but they came to see the play at Merrigong and made themselves known to me. Lance told me that Lindy's father was a great man who never said a bad word against anyone. Lance said that even when asked about the devil, Lindy's father said, 'Well, he's very hardworking'. I told this story to Lindy before we went onstage for a forum at the NLA and she laughed, delighted at this memory of her beloved father.

In Nowra, Lindy asked me to invite the Hatchmans to see the play at the Shoalhaven Entertainment Centre. In 1980 they lived next door to Lindy's parents, who did not have a telephone of their own, so it was on their phone that Lindy's parents received the call telling them that Azaria had been taken. I wrote to an old address from the files and was delighted when they replied that they would like to attend the show.

Kath Fisher, whose charming and very funny letters and poems were very gratefully received by Lindy during her time in jail, became a continuing source of amusement between Lindy and myself. The letters I wrote seeking her permission to use her poems came back 'return to sender' so I called every Kath Fisher I could find in the Yellow Pages. Then Rick Creighton, Lindy's husband, rang and said that Kath had written to Lindy via her website and left an email address … only the email bounced back when they tried to contact her. I tried as well but, alas, no luck. Then we did a story for *New Idea* around the time of the production of the play and, luckily, the journalist misspelt Kath's name

(I heard Lindy give it correctly). Kath again got in contact with Lindy and then with me. She generously gave full permission to use the letters and poems in this play—one of which Max Lambert expertly set to music for the beginning of Act Two.

The hardest email I have received during the research for this book and play was just days after we opened in Wollongong. John Kimber, the son of Gloria Kimber who wrote the wonderful 'Lullaby for Azaria', with which I end the play, wrote to tell me of his mother's death, only weeks before.

> 'It is with great sadness that I have to tell you that we lost our dear Mum, Gloria, on Monday 25th July at the age of 98 years. I am Gloria's eldest son, John. For the past 7 years I have been living in the family home as Mum's carer. I brought Mum home from hospital on Thursday and I am sorry to say that she slipped away before I was able to read her your letter (inviting her to the opening of the play). Mum would have been delighted with your news. She had not forgotten. From time to time she used to wonder how your play was progressing. Mum started writing plays, poems and short stories in her youth. She used to bring her troupe from her home town, Murray Bridge, to Adelaide to put on her plays. During the war she was Possum in the Childrens Pages of the *Sunday Mail*. Later she was editor of the Women's Pages. My two brothers, Robert and James, and I are lucky to have had such a loving mother of whom we can be so proud.'

I found a community in the 199 boxes of Mrs Chamberlain-Creighton's collection in the NLA and that that community is as diverse and contradictory and complex as any I have ever tried to understand. I would like to thank every person who took the trouble to sign my copyright clearance document and return it to me. If your letter is here and you have not heard from me, please write to me via the Harold White Fellows Room, National Library of Australia, Canberra ACT 2600.

I would like to acknowledge the staff at the National Library of Australia who awarded me a Harold White Fellowship in 2013—Margy Burn, Robyn Holmes, Catriona Anderson, Kylie Scroope and many others—you are the esteemed custodians of this precious bounty.

ACKNOWLEDGEMENTS

Thank you to Wesley Enoch and Bec Allen who were my referees for the successful NLA Fellowship Application. I have used only letters written to Mrs Chamberlain-Creighton though the collection contains many letters sent jointly to the Chamberlains and the rest of the family. I acknowledge their continuing pain and loss, which is largely outside the scope of my research. I thank Simon Hinton, Leland Kean and Merrigong Theatre Company who commissioned and produced *Letters to Lindy* and Darren Yap, Max Lambert, James Brown, Toby Knyvett, Sophie Fairweather and other production staff, and most of all the profoundly gifted cast—Jeanette Cronin, Glenn Hazeldine, Phillip Hinton and Jane Phegan. Thank you also to my agent Sharne McGee and to Vicki Gordon. Rick Creighton, thank you for your patient diligence, and Mrs Chamberlain-Creighton, Lindy, thank you for trusting me with your words, your precious collection and your generous wisdom.

On the night of the Wollongong opening, after the play, Lindy made a speech, much of which is reproduced in her foreword. When she finished she walked over to where I was standing, crying, and said: 'See, I got you back for all the crying in the play!' And then she embraced me.

Alana Valentine
December 2016

SETTING

The primary setting is an abstract re-creation of Lindy's home, her study or a spare bedroom, in which she is sorting through and filing all the 20,000 letters, photos, bookmarks and textcards she received from the public during her 35-year ordeal for deposit in the National Library of Australia. Some letters are filed, others are spilling out from boxes.

COSTUME

Because Lindy is both a qualified seamstress and a terrifically stylish person (and was exhaustively criticised for this), costume is extremely important to the central role. It is my hope that the character of Lindy will transform from her 1980s self to the woman who is finishing the filing in 2016. I imagine that clever costume changes can be effected with wigs and some of Lindy's iconic clothes. Differentiation between the letter-readers should be done carefully and entertainingly with costumes and props.

ENTRANCES & EXITS

Entrances and exits of the ensemble members are at the discretion of the director. The three ensemble cast members play letter-writers, other characters, and the chorus. In most cases there is time for the actors to go offstage and re-enter as a different character, though it is equally valid for them to remain continuously onstage and effect the change to another character either vocally or physically in view of the audience. Entrances and exits for Lindy are indicated in the stage directions but also may be adjusted by the director.

MUSIC

In the original Merrigong production, Kath Fisher's 'My Washing Isn't Omo Bright' was performed as an acapella chorus and set to music by Max Lambert, as was Gloria Kimber's 'Lullaby', which ends the play. I would urge producers to use Lambert's glorious music where possible, or to set these two works to music in any case. If you wish to use Lambert's music, contact Currency Press for details.

GRAMMAR & SPELLING

The letter extracts in the play are reproduced as faithfully as possible, including the particular grammar and spelling of the originals. My aim in doing so is to give readers, including potential theatre-makers, and our audiences, as authentic an experience of this historical archive as possible and indicates no judgement or comment on the letter-writers.

COURT TRANSCIPT

The court scene on pages 12–15 is transcript from the original trial of Lindy and Michael Chamberlain in 1982, on the public record.

HISTORICAL NAMES

The Central Australian monolith, Uluru, was commonly referred to as Ayers Rock in the early 1980s.

COPYRIGHT NOTE

Where possible, permission has been sought by the author from these copyright holders for clearance to use these letters in this play. In most cases permission has been obtained but, due to the age of some letters, in some cases the original letter writer has been uncontactable due to the address being out of date, anonymity or other reasons why the letter has become an 'orphan work' under the Copyright Act. Any letter-writer whom I have not been able to contact can write to me via the Harold White Fellows Room, National Library of Australia, Canberra ACT 2600.

DIGITAL IMAGES

Digital images of some of these letters (and many others from the collection) appear in Alana Valentine's *Dear Lindy*, published by the National Library of Australia in 2017. A useful timeline of events associated with the Chamberlains' ordeal also appears in that publication.

CHARACTERS

LINDY CHAMBERLAIN-CREIGHTON

FIGURE 1, female, any age; doubles as: ANONYMOUS (letter-writer), NOLAN, ROFF, PHILLIPS, VALERIE THOMSON, MAY, CHRISTINE GEORGE, ROSLYN, INMATE, LILY, GUARD, KATH FISHER, MAVIS, JENNY, GREG, GORDON, SUSAN, GAYLE HANNAH, BARBARA, ELIZABETH MORRIS.

FIGURE 2, male, any age; doubles as: ANONYMOUS (letter-writer), JUDY, BARRITT, CAMERON, SCOTT, JAMES THOMSON, RONALD, MAN, GUARD, GLENDON, AIDAN, MALCOLM BROWN, NEIL, LIBRARIAN, GLORIA KIMBER.

FIGURE 3, male, any age; doubles as: ANONYMOUS (letter-writer), GOODWIN, BROWN, SCOTT, BARKER, PAULA, JAMES DRAM, SECURITY, MAN, REAGAN, MIKE, HELEN, LIBRARIAN.

ACT ONE

2016. LINDY *enters, carrying a box of letters.*

ANONYMOUS [FIGURE 1]: Hello, murderers.

ANONYMOUS [FIGURE 2]: I am sending you a photo, I thought you would like to see and frame and keep on your dressing table to remind you of the days of murdering the baby you always say you didn't.

ANONYMOUS [FIGURE 3]: What a pack of lies.

ANONYMOUS [FIGURE 1]: Read this out to your kids and let them know what people thought of you.

ANONYMOUS [FIGURE 2]: Don't think it has all died down, far from it.

ANONYMOUS [FIGURE 3]: Are you still borrowing clothes from other people?

ANONYMOUS [FIGURE 1]: Why didn't you put this lovely photo of you on this lovely book you have written and let you see what you looked like at that time instead of the stuck-up-looking bitch you are now?

ANONYMOUS [FIGURE 2]: Fancy coming on TV and saying what you do, you ought to hang your head in shame.

ALL: Yours truly.

ANONYMOUS [FIGURE 3]: Actress Lindy, if you are so poor, why have you got so many clothes?

ANONYMOUS [FIGURE 2]: Killing Azaria made you a millionaire.

ANONYMOUS [FIGURE 1]: You're so bloody hard, no tears have ever come out of your eyes.

ANONYMOUS [FIGURE 3]: But the eldest boy probably made the first nick into poor little Azaria's throat and you had to do the rest, don't you think you have enough of Australian taxpayers' money? And by the reading you reckon another kid is going to die by a dingo, are you going to do that job too?

ANONYMOUS [FIGURE 2]: Judge Morling didn't find you innocent did he, he left the case opened. I hope one day you'll be punished and that husband of yours.

ANONYMOUS [FIGURE 1]: I would not walk across the road to see the film because it shows us what a bad-tempered bitch you are, no wonder

Australia hates the movie where did the blood come from poor little Azaria I could not kill a kitten but your murder was premeditated because you studied the life of dingoes fancy describing seven different dingoes in your trials.

ANONYMOUS [FIGURE 3]: You're a cunning bitch and will always be one get out of Australia when your [sic] rich and famous.

ANONYMOUS [FIGURE 2]: Imelda Marcos eat your heart out.

ALL: Disgusted.

ANONYMOUS [FIGURE 1]: Lindy, for the sake of the poor wee mite, if you both know her resting place show where it is, don't leave her to lie in the wilderness. Please I offer a plea from Azaria.

ANONYMOUS [FIGURE 2]: I gazed with an infant's
    smiling trust,

ANONYMOUS [FIGURE 3]: that
    was changed to shocked
    surprise.

ANONYMOUS [FIGURE 1]: And as death glazed my
    dying eyes I cried—

ALL: Why? Why must I die!

ANONYMOUS [FIGURE 2]: Still my restless spirit
    cries from my unmarked
    grave, Sighing—
    Why … oh why?!

ALL: From an annoyed decent person.

ANONYMOUS [FIGURE 3]: You murdered Azaria and your husband knew you planned the murder because you made a black dress to bury her. You both should be ashamed of yourselves. Some witnesses of yours should be charged with telling lies.

No dog or dingo was involved. Just you too [sic]. God will punish you both. The welfare should take all your kids away from you as your sons will hate you both in years to come they won't trust you as they know you are liars.

Thou shalt not kill. Dozen dingoes were also shot for your lies. Azaria won't rest in peace because her mother was too weak to tell the truth.

You made a lot of money from your baby's death and now you are using your new baby to get out of prison. You both belong to Satan.

You are not Christians. You are both weak. Stop using young babies to get your own way. Better people are still in prison not using the public for money also the media for money. You both should grow up and work for your living.

LINDY: I thought we'd start with the comic relief. Yeah. That's what I used to call the nasty letters. Because I must have received, oh, at least twenty thousand letters just up to the point of when I got out of jail, and then more afterwards and then all the emails of course. I'm still getting about one thousand emails a year. Two out of three are apologies. But the nasty ones were always just a bit different. Some of them even gave me the giggles, I got the giggles with Meryl Streep over one of them because there was a woman who wrote and told me she wouldn't spend any time on me and wouldn't be supporting me. Meryl got an identical letter and in both of them she sent a black bootie with red ribbons. So Meryl asked me if I would like hers to have a pair and I said sure. This woman who said she wouldn't spend any time on me actually provided me with a lovely pair of black booties. So.

LINDY *is now holding a lovely pair of black booties, with red trim.*

MARILYN NOLAN [FIGURE 1]: 17th February 1986.

Dear Lindy,

My thoughts have been with you for many years now and I do apologise for not writing to you before this. I have always felt a special bond with you from the first day I met you—in the Mount Isa Maternity Ward—in the private bathroom—on the 12th June 1980. Azaria and Elisha were both born the day before. I cannot forget your kindness to me whilst I was in hospital and both my mother (Di Collins who has also recently written to you) and I have never forgotten your intense joy in your daughter Azaria.

I have also never forgotten your very true and intense grief at the memorial in Mount Isa for Azaria. You were trying to be fairly composed when you were greeting all the people leaving the church after the memorial and then you saw me and we both broke down and hugged each other.

Lindy, I don't think you know that I was a Detective in the Mount Isa CI Branch prior to having Elisha and over the years I had personally dealt with Child Abusers and the like and also murderers.

I always had a special knack of knowing whether or not a person was guilty of what they were accused of (whether they confessed to it or not) and in all cases I dealt with I was proved right.

And that is why, since the 17th August 1980, I have always (I have never once wavered in my thinking) said, to as many people who would listen, that there was no way in the world that you murdered your daughter.

Azaria and yourself are never far from my thoughts—each birthday for Elisha is both a happy and sad occasion for me, because Elisha is a constant reminder of Azaria.

Kindest regards,
Marilyn Nolan.

LINDY: She came round and saw me soon after we got back, soon after it happened, after she was taken. And that's why she sort of 'fessed up all those years later. She came round with the baby and beforehand they asked me and they were thinking they should leave it behind and I said no, bring her. They were born on exactly the same day, so her little Elisha was exactly the same size as Azaria would have been. Still only very small.

JUDY [FIGURE 2]: 3 Oct, 1980.

Please forgive me for not writing to you before this. I have tried to ring you but no answer—I'm afraid we are so isolated that until we heard the TV news last night we had imagined that the forensic report findings had closed the case of Azaria's death, and we had no idea of what you must be undergoing.

LINDY *exits.*

We had never spoken to anyone (the police or the media) about the night of Azaria's death since it had always seemed so totally and irrevocably true that she was taken by a dingo, and the possibility that it could be questioned—however remotely—simply didn't arise. Anything we could have contributed would have been unnecessary. However, after hearing the latest news and reading the *Woman's Day* I realised how appalling gossip and innuendo can be, so I am writing to say that if there is anything we can do or say to help we will do so with all our heart.

And perhaps telling you why we were so utterly convinced that the

ACT ONE

dingo had taken the baby will help. Being camped within feet of your tent and with the night so still and clear meant that Bill, Catherine and I were aware of what was happening maybe more than most people around.

First I must say that both Bill and I heard the dingo growl. We've a labrador dog at home who gives the same kind of growl and we both heard it (and noted it for the same reason) without commenting at the time. I don't remember hearing the baby crying—I guess because it would be a sort of ordinary sound that I wouldn't bother to register.

1980. LINDY *enters in a sundress.*

The next thing I was aware of was you, Lindy, crying something like, 'O God, the dingo's got my baby'. And I simply couldn't believe my ears—in fact the whole idea seemed so completely incredible that we were stunned. Almost literally. And then everyone started moving with torches. Bill moved the car to shine the lights into the sandhills and then he and Catherine drove down to tell the police. Please let us know if there is anything that we could possibly do to help in any way. With love,

Judy and Bill and Catherine.

LINDY: Judy and Bill were key witnesses in the trial of course. They were in the tent next door. They never wavered, they never flinched from insisting that the dingo took Azaria. Never. Nobody who was actually there ever did.

So let's start at the beginning then:
I'd put Azaria down in the tent to sleep
returned to the barbeque area
when Michael and the others with us, heard the baby cry out.
So when I went to check on her I saw a dingo,
a wild dog, coming out of the tent with something in its mouth and I called out,
'The dingo's got my baby'.
It's a statement of fact.
And it's very clear.
I know now that it's considered too clear.
Apparently it would have been more believable if I had
choked, hysterical,

'In the tent ... a ... a ... get out ...'
Oh, I know what they would have liked,
'Get away from her,
Get away, you,
Get away from my baby'.
They wouldn't have made fun of that.
'Oh God, Oh God, Oh God!'
Or just a blood-curdling scream
and instant tears.
But that's not what I do
that's not going to help
I thought of the baby not myself
I didn't get emotional or hysterical
because I wasn't thinking of myself
I was thinking there might still be a chance
so I give the news as clearly and precisely as I can,
'A dingo's got my baby'.
So that they don't have to waste time on
'What is it? What's happened? What's wrong?'
I just screwed it all up into what's happened
and how and the race to fix it.
Because you're in it
it's happening
and she's gone
and you can't undo it
and you can't unlose her
and you can't for a moment
indulge your feelings
so you yell,
'The dingo's got my baby!'
And that's where it begins.

FIGURE 2: Statement of Wallace Victor Goodwin:

GOODWIN [FIGURE 3]: About the 16th August, 1980, in company with my wife, two children and mother in law, we set out on a camping holiday to Ayers Rock and Alice Springs via the Flinders Ranges.

On Thursday, the 21st August, 1980, we arrived at Ayers Rock, around twelve midday. We set up two tents, a twelve by nine and nine by nine, in the camping area adjacent to a bus camping area.

Together with the family, I visited the Ayers Rock, carried out the normal tourist activities. We then found our way across to the Maggie Springs area. We then left and drove around what I know as the Mossface area which has a natural water catchment area at the base of the Rock. Myself, my wife, and the two children walked into this particular area. Margot, my wife, and daughter, Jo-Ann, were climbing over rocks to the right of me and my wife said to me, 'What's that in front of you?' At this point of time, my son, Phillip, and I were following an animal track which we followed from the tree line in towards the base of the Rock. On reaching the end of the animal track and rounding a boulder, I could see a disposable nappy scattered around within an eighteen to twenty inch diameter. Within this diameter was also the jump suit and singlet.

I knelt down to make a closer examination, and at this time my wife, Margot, and son, Phillip, walked over to where I was and at that time I pushed Phillip back out of the way and I said, 'It's the baby's clothes'. Jo-Anne cried out and Margot went over to comfort her, and took the two children back to the car. I then proceeded further into the Rock. There was a cave. I knelt down and looked inside. I could not see anything. I made a further examination of the nearby area and then went back to where the clothing was.

The grow suit was lying on its back, with the feet facing up in the air, which gave the appearance of the lower part of the leg and feet still being in it. I noticed that the clips on the grow suit were open from the neck right through to the leg, and including the left leg. I would explain that the suit was somewhat crumpled, but it did expose the singlet inside the grow suit as far down as the waist. The feet were facing out towards the road, and the top of the jump suit towards the rock itself. One thing I did notice was that the outside of the rear of the nappy was facing upwards, and the napkin still contained a certain amount of filler. The nappy was just touching the grow suit in the vicinity of the legs area. I noticed that the neck area of the grow suit was badly bloodstained. I did not observe any vegetation or soil stuck to the bloodied area of the jump suit, nor did I for that matter notice any vegetation or soil on any other part of the grow suit.

FIGURE 1: Coroner Denis Barritt:

BARRITT [FIGURE 2]: I find that Azaria Chantel Lauren Chamberlain, a child then of nine weeks of age and formerly of Mount Isa, Queensland, met her death when attacked by a wild dingo whilst asleep in the family's tent at the top camping area, Ayers Rock, shortly after 8 p.m. on 17 August, 1980.

I find further that in attempting to remove this baby from the tent, the dingo would have caused severe crushing to the base of the skull and neck and lacerations to the throat and neck. Such injuries would have resulted in swift death.

I further find that neither of the parents of the child, nor either of their remaining children were in any degree whatsoever responsible for this death.

I find that that the name Azaria does not mean and never has meant 'sacrifice in the wilderness'. I find that after her death the body of Azaria was taken from the possession of the dingo and disposed of by an unknown method, by a person or persons unknown.

ROFF [FIGURE 1]: 25th February, 1981.

I am writing to pass on to you and your children the best wishes of the staff of Uluru National Park.

Both I and my ranger staff are sorry that your visit to this park in August 1980 resulted in such a tragedy as the loss of your daughter which also led to the long period of suspicion and gossip that you were all subjected to by ill-informed people. I am glad that the inquest hearing exonerated you and I hope and trust that you will be permitted to live in happiness and peace and that your traumatic experience is over, although I realise that the events of 17th August will remain with you all forever.

May I and my wife Roberta and our children extend our sympathy and the hope for a happy future to you all.

Yours sincerely,
Derek Roff,
Senior Park Ranger,
Ayers Rock.

The FIGURES *become a chorus and circle* LINDY, *whispering.*

FIGURE 1: A dingo couldn't do this thing
          It doesn't have a truthful ring

ACT ONE

FIGURE 2: Can't run with such heavy weight
   The child has had a darker fate
FIGURE 3: Adventists practise sacrifice
   An infant is the going price
FIGURE 1: She dressed in black this little kid
   And named her for the deed they did
FIGURE 2: Their Bible's underlined in gore
   A coffin's in their garage store
FIGURE 3: And look at how she doesn't grieve
   She's way too calm to be believed.
LINDY: Kenneth Brown is a forensic dentist, and a Seventh Day Adventist. An Adventist dentist. He tells police that the cuts in the clothes were not made by dingoes and he sends the clothing to the UK. To a Professor James Cameron. He shares a name with the James Cameron who made *Titanic* and *Terminator* and *Aliens*. And James Cameron has a lurid imagination. The filmmaker, I mean, of course.
BROWN [FIGURE 3]: I've done tests with dingoes in Adelaide Zoo
   And the cuts on the clothing just won't do
   They were not made by dingo teeth
   And there's no saliva underneath.
ALL: We've come to make a threat of death
FIGURE 1: You don't deserve to still draw breath
ALL: We've come to bomb your hotel room
FIGURE 2: You traitor to your sex and womb
ALL: The media report each day
FIGURE 3: There's nowhere you can get away
ALL: Why don't you sob, why don't you cry?
FIGURE 1: We know that you're just full of lies
ALL: Look at your pretty, handmade clothes
FIGURE 2: You've got no right to dress in those
ALL: I don't know what's in that legal book
FIGURE 3: But I know you've got a guilty look.
LINDY: We kept getting more and more letters and many them were describing in detail what dingoes were capable of.
SCOTT [FIGURE 2]: My experience has been that dingoes have very little natural fear of humans, but if hunted they soon learn to fear man.
LINDY: Men who had built the rabbit-proof fence or stored meat in out-

door meat safes.

SCOTT [FIGURE 3]: Out in the mustering camps, grilling steak at night attracts dingoes like a magnet. In dingo-infested country it is common to see their eyes reflected in the firelight.

LINDY: But others said that a dingo couldn't carry a ten-pound animal. That there had to be another explanation. A darker explanation. One that involved nail scissors.

And a woman who could decapitate her own child with nail scissors.

And a mother who had given birth and dressed her in a lemon-trimmed matinee jacket and then ... hacked her head off with nail scissors.

With nail scissors.

I know I keep saying nail scissors.

I know we need to move forward now but I can't quite move beyond nail scissors.

Do you know how small nail scissors are?

Not supposed to focus on the nail scissors.

Supposed to be horrified by the idea of cutting, the idea of decapitating.

Supposed to cry a little and grimace a lot about blood and skin and mess.

I didn't even use nail scissors, silly man, I used nail clippers.

But going round and round and round on the nail scissors theory, well, the pair they found later fell in half when they went to test them and there was no blood on them.

But the letter-writers were very keen on describing what would happen if I had cut my baby's throat with nail scissors.

SCOTT [FIGURE 2]: Dear Lindy,

If anyone believes that it is possible to kill a ten-pound animal of any description in the front seat of a small car without getting soaked in blood they should try it on a ten-pound suckling pig, having first tied its legs. I have slaughtered hundreds, if not thousands of animals and I know that I couldn't. Cutting a jugular vein is like a burst garden hose—blood squirts everywhere.

SCOTT [FIGURE 3]: When the throat is cut or the head severed of a fowl, duck or pullet [*about the size comparison with Azaria*] the blood spurts out—mostly just runs down over the breast and stomach feathers, therefore to avoid getting blood all over the hands of the person plucking the poultry, the object is held up for some seconds by its legs with its neck section down almost to the ground causing a largish or smaller pool of blood on the ground.

LINDY: I started putting all the letters in this file. And it was kind of like 'You've got nothing left so this is part of her'. I mean, there was nothing else, so the letters became …

Pause.

FIGURE 1: The rumours continue to fly
FIGURE 2: Conjecture about who and why
FIGURE 3: We drag a plastic doll of her
ALL: To show how baby clothes catch dirt
FIGURE 1: Dismantle plumbing where you stayed
FIGURE 2: Detectives in a hotel raid
FIGURE 3: Imagine bones in the pipes and drains
ALL: We hope for tell-tale red blood stains
ALL: We seize your family car to test
FIGURE 1: We want another full inquest
FIGURE 2: And Operation Ochre's name
FIGURE 3: Comes from the desert where we claim
ALL: You took the body of your little child
And cut her throat with a reckless smile.

A fan above the stage begins to slowly turn.

LINDY: The night before I went into the witness box. As soon as I went into this room, this room where we were staying in Darwin, I thought, 'There's something in here'. We were in Darwin, it was roasting, there was air-conditioning in this room but it didn't go very low. But in this room I went into … it was like walking into a room with the freezer turned on. And the minute I walked in all the hairs on the back of my neck stood up. When I turned the light on there was nothing there. Michael had gone out to the other room. And so I turned the light out again, and that's when something heavy pushed on my chest to choke me. And I thought immediately, 'This is what my dad has described when he'd worked with people who thought they had evil in their house'. All I could think of was that he or somebody had said, 'If you repeat God's name then it will go'. But to begin with I could not even formulate the word in my head. I had to really fight until I could say it in my mind and then out loud and then I could move again and then I could say it louder and louder and I grabbed my Bible which was beside me and held onto it. From then on I slept with my Bible under my pillow. Sometimes I'd go into that room and I'd start to feel it and then I'd grab the Bible and it would go. And as I said Jesus' name over and over again the temperature of the room started to rise, the weight came off me and I could breathe again.

If you can't or won't or you don't want to believe me that's your prerogative. But you don't have to believe in physical evil the way I do to try to understand the evil that was being done in the world around me. There is evil that is supernatural and there is evil that is injustice. Well, that injustice tried to choke me to death. It was newsprint. It was the words you whispered or gossiped or the jokes you made. All of that balled up and became injustice. This grotesque series of lies and spite and rumour and human evil tried to smother my sense of belief in good and had me by the throat. Don't deny that it happened to me. Whatever name you give it, if it ever has you by the throat, let's talk again afterwards.

The fan stops.

FIGURE 2: September and October, 1982.
FIGURE 1: Ian Barker QC:
BARKER [FIGURE 3]: A baby was killed at Ayers Rock on 17 August 1980, during the evening between eight and nine o'clock. She died very quickly because somebody had cut her throat. The Crown does not venture to suggest any reason or motive for the killing. It is not part of our case that Mrs Chamberlain had previously shown any ill will toward the child. Nor do we assert that the child was other than a normal baby. The Crown does not, therefore, attempt to prove motive, nor does it invite speculation as to motive. We simply say to you that the evidence put before you will prove beyond reasonable doubt that, for whatever reason, the baby was murdered by her mother. Shortly after the event, the mother asserted, and thereafter continued to assert, that the dead child had been taken from the tent by a dingo. The Crown says that the dingo story was a fanciful lie, calculated to conceal the

truth, which is that the child Azaria died by her mother's hand.
CAMERON [FIGURE 2]: I saw no evidence on any of these garments to suggest that any member of the canine family was involved.
LINDY: James Cameron.
CAMERON [FIGURE 2]: I cannot say anything about dingoes. I speak about the canine family in general.
BARKER [FIGURE 3]: In your opinion, is there evidence suggesting to you that the child was not killed by a member of the canine family?
CAMERON [FIGURE 2]: There is evidence to suggest it was killed in another method. It suggests there was an incised wound around the neck. In other words, a cut throat.
BARKER [FIGURE 3]: Caused by?
CAMERON [FIGURE 2]: A cutting instrument across the neck, or around the neck.
BARKER [FIGURE 3]: Held by?
CAMERON [FIGURE 2]: Held by a human element.

    LINDY *exits.*

BARKER [FIGURE 3]: What do you say about the possibility of a dog or a dingo having savaged the child in the head?
CAMERON [FIGURE 2]: I do not think there is enough evidence on the jumpsuit, alone, to support that theory.
BARKER [FIGURE 3]: What happens if a dog bites a child's head?
CAMERON [FIGURE 2]: A lot depends on where, on the head, it bites. It would be very difficult for me to imagine a dog grasping the head from above. That would be the only way in which I think a dog could possibly grasp a child without damaging the collar. But, in so doing, I would have expected extensive bleeding, but not around the collar of the jumpsuit.
BARKER [FIGURE 3]: Why?
CAMERON [FIGURE 2]: Because when you get a head injury, you get rivulets of blood draining down, and missing the collar. It goes down the front and down the back. Depending on which way the head is bending, certainly, you'll get bleeding around the back of the collar, depending on how the child lay afterwards, where there's pooling of blood. I would have anticipated that it could only be described by a cut-throat type of injury.

BARKER [FIGURE 3]: Had the child been lifted and moved by a dog, what do you say about saliva?

CAMERON [FIGURE 2]: I would have anticipated saliva from any member of the canine family lifting a garment ...

> PHILLIPS [FIGURE 1] *comes to cross-examine. 1982.* LINDY *re-enters, visibly pregnant.*

PHILLIPS [FIGURE 1]: A nappy was one of the articles found by Mr Goodwin?

CAMERON [FIGURE 2]: Yes.

PHILLIPS [FIGURE 1]: He referred to 'a nappy lying next to it', that is the suit, 'with a few tear-marks in it, and the plastic liner, with the insides exposed'.

CAMERON [FIGURE 2]: Yes.

PHILLIPS [FIGURE 1]: Did you say this, in your report, and I will just read the material part now: 'Suffice to say I have never known a member of the canine family pulling off a nappy intact'. That is what you reported, was it not?

CAMERON [FIGURE 2]: That is correct, yes.

PHILLIPS [FIGURE 1]: You reported that without seeing the photographs of the scene?

CAMERON [FIGURE 2]: Yes.

PHILLIPS [FIGURE 1]: On the basis of what Doctor Brown told you?

CAMERON [FIGURE 2]: No, the appearance of the nappy when I examined it ...

PHILLIPS [FIGURE 1]: You indicated an area, which was on an ultraviolet photograph of the back of the suit, and pointed to 'a possible, more diffuse area there which gives the impression to me of the heel of the hand, with extended fingers'. Right?

CAMERON [FIGURE 2]: Yes. I corrected it, and said it wasn't the heel. It was that part of the hand.

PHILLIPS [FIGURE 1]: And referring to other marks you suggest 'they could be the fingers of the right hand', but you couldn't be dogmatic about it.

CAMERON [FIGURE 2]: Correct.

PHILLIPS [FIGURE 1]: So we are talking of impressions of impressions, and suggestions based thereon, are we not, Professor? Or, more to the point, that is what you are talking about?'

ACT ONE 15

CAMERON [FIGURE 2]: That is a play on words.
PHILLIPS [FIGURE 1]: Well, they are your words.
CAMERON [FIGURE 2]: And they are my impressions.
VALERIE THOMSON [FIGURE 1]: 9th October, 1982.
Dear Lindy,
I imagine that you had a rough week last week. I hope the worst is over for you now. I realise what a nightmare it has been for you both. Once would have been bad enough but this is the third time. We picked up Aidan and Reagan after lunch and they have had a great time playing in the clay at the back of the dam. As usual their sandshoes and socks were wet through. Aidan was about to strip off for a swim in the dam when I reminded them both that it was time to go home to Grandma. I won't tell you what Aidan said! A good time was had by all! I will close off now. I know the Lord is with you, just a few more weeks and this trial will be over and done with for good.
Valerie Thomson.
JAMES THOMSON [FIGURE 2]: 24th September 1982.
Dear Lindy,
How are things? I presume you know me, James Thomson is my name if you don't. Hope you are feeling well because I am. Before you left I told you I would probably be on my 'P's' when you get back but from what I hear you'll be back here much sooner than we thought. It's a nice night down here and I know that you are having a nice night also. Hopefully it will be a good day tomorrow. I must let you go but remember we are all thinking of you and I know that you will all be back with us very soon. I am looking forward to that very much.
Goodbye for now,
James Thomson.
PAULA [FIGURE 3]: Dear Mrs Chamberlain,
I hope you're feeling well. I think of you very often. We all believe in you. We give you all the hope we've got. There are a lot of people who would love to be your friend. What ever I can send or give you that will help with your appeal I am going to empty my money box and purse, pillow and send it to you all the love, kindness and helpfulness I can give to you and your family. My Brother's and Sisters are well. There [sic] names are Jackie, Danelle, Damien There are two girls and a boy. Jackie is five, Danelle is two, Damien

is eleven, I'm Paula I'm nine. There are eight people Mum, Dad, Jackie, Danelle, Damien, Me, Grandma and my Uncle David we all live in the same house. We live in the bush. It's fun the main animals we find are Koalas, Kangaroos, Wallabies and frilly necked lizard. We have a puppy a cat we had a guinea pig but it died we are going to get another one when we get the cage fixed. I hope you like my letter. Please write back to me I'll write again when I get your letter. Don't forget the love that I am giving you.
Love From Paula,
Age nine.

MAY [FIGURE 1]: Dear Lindy,

Hi! I am a part-Aboriginal girl. I want you to know that I am on your side, and I believe that you are INNOCENT!

There were a lot said against in the Media, and I know the bloody Media exaggerates, what they say about Aborigines, all aren't true.

My elders have told me stories about dingoes (wild) being nearly attacked by them, mind you these were grown-ups (dingoes aren't scared of humans—when they're hungry).

I hope this letter is not disgusting you. Domestic dogs, even attack their own masters.

We're on your side, Lindy.

Love,

May.

LINDY: I mean, there was nothing else, so the letters became ...

Pause.

They tried to make a fool of Nipper, the Aboriginal tracker, in court by commenting on his glasses. I mean, he wore Coke-bottle-bottom glasses so they were like he can't see, ha ha, how would he know. And yet when the journalist, Kevin Hitchcock, went out there he said they were all there with Nipper and someone was coming from down the road and he didn't have his glasses on and they couldn't see who it was because he was still too far off and Nipper said, 'Oh, that fella coming', and it was one of their mates that they didn't even know had got to the Rock yet. So there was nothing wrong with his sight.

The big thing with his testimony was that he said, 'I did this' and 'I did that', and as soon as he'd go out they'd say well it was patently obvious he didn't do those things because he wasn't there till the next day. What they didn't say was that in traditional lore, as head man he has the right to say 'I' for every person in the tribe and he was saying 'I' for Barbara and Daisy and Captain Number Two. So that night Captain Number Two was tracking and Nipper was saying, 'I was there'. So that was a lot of confusion and I didn't even understand that myself for a long while.

When they questioned Barbara, one of the Aboriginal trackers, she said, 'I tell you true,' and she said, 'I talk one way, you talk the other, you lie'. To Barker, the Prosecutor. He went all colours and he tried all sorts of ways to get her to say something and every time she'd say, 'No, I told you true'. And even Morling, when he was writing his report for the Royal Commission, asked her, 'Could it have been a joey?', and Barbara said to him, 'Was there a joey living in the tent?' Poor Morling went fiery red. It was like she thought, 'How stupid can you be? Stupid white man.'

Finally the translator says, 'You've got to understand, these people, when you leave this place, can tell you exactly where each person goes. When they are children and they want their mothers they aren't told where she is, their relative or someone in their mob points at tracks on the ground and says, "Go find Mummy, that's her footprint". That's why they are so good at observing and tracking.'

ALL: During a period of between five and ten minutes:

FIGURE 2: Mrs Chamberlain is alleged to have gone with Azaria and her son, Aiden, from the barbecue area to their tent some twenty to thirty metres away; donned tracksuit pants over her dress; taken Azaria from the tent to the family car which was parked alongside; slit Azaria's throat with a sharp instrument (possibly nail scissors) while sitting in the front passenger seat of the car; hidden the body (possibly in a camera bag in the car); returned to the tent with blood on her hands and the tracksuit pants; removed the tracksuit pants and washed her hands in an ice-cream container; and returned, composed, to the barbecue area with Aiden who has witnessed this entire scenario.

ALL: Or:

FIGURE 3: As Mrs Chamberlain claimed, a dingo took the baby.

FIGURE 1: But there was no blood on the bassinet.

FIGURE 3: No trail of blood was seen leading from the tent.

FIGURE 1: And the tracksuit pants, belonging to Mrs Chamberlain, were sent by her for dry-cleaning at Mount Isa. The marks on the tracksuit pants were on the front and below the knee; the stains, or spots, appeared to be splattered or flicked on, and tapered off in size towards the bottom of the pants.

FIGURE 2: The Crown case is that Mrs Chamberlain must have been wearing the pants when she committed the murder.

ALL: Or:

FIGURE 3: The blood might have dropped onto the pants while they were lying folded in the tent.

FIGURE 1: According to the evidence of Mrs Chamberlain, the baby had also been wearing a jacket, but no jacket was found. Soil, and fragments of vegetation, were found on the jumpsuit, and there was scientific evidence which entitled the jury to infer that the clothes had been buried, not near where they were found, but in an area with a different type of soil—one place that answered the description was under bushes on the side of the sand dunes about a hundred metres from the camp.

ALL: The learned trial judge directed the jury as follows:

FIGURE 2: If you are satisfied that blood was found in the family car, even if you have a doubt that it was foetal blood, you're still entitled to ask yourselves how that blood came to be there.

If you find because of the location of blood in the car that it cannot be explained, you can still consider whether it was Azaria's blood—that is the only explanation available after you—after you consider the other evidence.

LINDY: The jury found that the slit throat, camera bag, tracksuit, entirely motiveless murder of my daughter was proved, beyond reasonable doubt.

FIGURE 3: *Daily Telegraph*, February 9, 1986.

FIGURE 2: By James Oram, who has covered the Chamberlain case since the first inquest:

JAMES DRAM [FIGURE 3]: ... And then Justice Muirhead was saying the words: 'Alice Lynne Chamberlain, you have been found guilty of murder by verdict of a jury. There is only one sentence I can pass upon you with the law of this Territory and that is imprisonment with hard labour for life.' Later that night, in a Darwin nightclub, crowded hot and thick with smoke, the disco records stopped playing while an announcement was made: 'The dingo didn't do it', and everyone cheered. I will always remember that, the cheering from people who were probably kind to their kids, good to their pets, and wouldn't harm anyone. Good, ordinary people.

Yet they cheered because a woman was going to jail for life.

I left and walked through the deserted streets of Darwin, thinking about the case and why it had affected all of Australia, divided the nation into those supporting the dingo theory and those who saw her as a monster.

CHRISTINE GEORGE [FIGURE 1]: October 30, 1982.

5.40 a.m.

Dearest Lindy,

I feel compelled to write to you to tell you how stunned we all are at the verdict. A life sentence. It doesn't seem possible. I don't know if this letter will even reach you; I hope so because I want you to know you are a very special person and very close to our hearts. We met together with your Mum and Dad last night to have a special prayer on your behalf.

Lindy we can't understand why—this whole thing has been one long nightmare—but I remember you told me once about that frog in the bucket of cream that kept swimming and turned that cream into butter. Keep swimming, honey! Even though right now your fight must be almost snuffed out, I know you are made of very special stuff.

Monday November 1

12.45 a.m.

Well, what a weekend it has been—so many tears shed by everyone but such a fantastic spirit of unity of church that I have never felt before. Lindy it hasn't all been in vain if your suffering helps us as a church to forget our differences and love one another more, then it hasn't all been for nothing. It was all so emotional, so moving and all because of you, Lindy, my dear little friend!

Yesterday I called around to see your folks. Your Mum was still really distraught as of course she would be. If you could you would be the one comforting her; I know that. I had Aidan and Reagan for the day. They were as good as gold. Aidan had one little outburst but he's got so much to be angry about. With love, and firmness, he'll be fine.

As for your little son, Reagan, he's an absolute darling, so gentle and cuddly. He played with Rachael and together they weeded Pauline's garden—did a really good job too. Pauline paid them both and they were happy. Pauline gave them both a hair trim—they looked really good too. Today they are coming home with my two from school and I'll run them home—a hide and seek game with the press!

Till next time lots of love, all my prayers and many thoughts of you. Keep up your courage and remember all of those who love you and believe in you.

Lots of love,

Christine.

LINDY: Nineteen days after I went to jail

Kahlia Shonell Nikari Chamberlain was born in Darwin Hospital on November 17, 1982.

I fought to hold her inside me.
Because as soon as she was born, one hour later she
would be taken from me.
Because I was dangerous.
I wouldn't even be permitted to see her on family visits
until she was one year old.
Then she would apparently be out of danger
from me.
So I fought the contractions.
Which made them hurt twice as much.
The body does what the mind wants.
The body refuses to release the child from inside.
The body holds
and holds
and holds on
until it can't hold on any longer.
When she was born she had a little double chin and a
round belly.
My biggest baby.
Four days later they let me out on bail
And in the Territory they printed T-shirts:
'Watch out, Kahlia, Mummy's coming home'.

LINDY *exits.*

ACT ONE

SCENE: LABOUR WARD, DARWIN HOSPITAL.

ROSLYN [FIGURE 1]: These are for Mrs Chamberlain.

SECURITY [FIGURE 3]: No.

ROSLYN [FIGURE 1]: Oh, I don't want to see her, I just want them to be passed onto her.

SECURITY [FIGURE 3]: No.

ROSLYN [FIGURE 1]: No, you won't pass them on to her?

SECURITY [FIGURE 3]: No.

ROSLYN [FIGURE 1]: Oh, you think there's something in them, other than flowers?

He inspects them.

SECURITY [FIGURE 3]: No.

ROSLYN [FIGURE 1]: Could you please say something other than no?

Pause.

SECURITY [FIGURE 3]: No.

ROSLYN [FIGURE 1]: Her room is already full of flowers. Let me guess, no.

SECURITY [FIGURE 3]: Could you move away now, madam.

ROSLYN [FIGURE 1]: He speaks.

SECURITY [FIGURE 3]: Listen, luv, I'm just doing my job. You can't give the flowers to Mrs Chamberlain. She is a prisoner of the Northern Territory and whether she's had a baby or not she is not allowed to receive gifts, presents, letters, cards or flowers.

ROSLYN [FIGURE 1]: She's just had a baby.

SECURITY [FIGURE 3]: Lots of women have babies.

ROSLYN [FIGURE 1]: Pretty obvious that you've never had a baby.

SECURITY [FIGURE 3]: Pretty obvious that you've never been arrested.

ROSLYN [FIGURE 1]: Oh, that will make a great headline: 'Woman arrested for trying to deliver flowers'.

SECURITY [FIGURE 3]: I'm asking you, politely, to please leave.

ROSLYN [FIGURE 1]: The baby is going to be taken away from her. You're taking away from her the only thing she wants, so why not just pass on these flowers.

SECURITY [FIGURE 3]: Because it's not allowed.

ROSLYN [FIGURE 1]: Are you made of stone?
SECURITY [FIGURE 3]: Clearly.
ROSLYN [FIGURE 1]: Would you like them?
SECURITY [FIGURE 3]: Absolutely not.
ROSLYN [FIGURE 1]: I can't take them back home. Please take them.
SECURITY [FIGURE 3]: What part of 'absolutely' don't you understand?
ROSLYN [FIGURE 1]: Give them to your wife. Sounds like she needs them.
SECURITY [FIGURE 3]: You want to get personal?
ROSLYN [FIGURE 1]: What?
SECURITY [FIGURE 3]: Are you a member of Mrs Chamberlain's family?
ROSLYN [FIGURE 1]: No.
SECURITY [FIGURE 3]: Are you a friend of hers?
ROSLYN [FIGURE 1]: No.
SECURITY [FIGURE 3]: Friend of the family?
ROSLYN [FIGURE 1]: No.
SECURITY [FIGURE 3]: Then why don't you mind your own business?
ROSLYN [FIGURE 1]: …
SECURITY [FIGURE 3]: You read about her in the paper and you think, 'I'll go and give that woman flowers, just to show how kind I am'.
ROSLYN [FIGURE 1]: That's not why.
SECURITY [FIGURE 3]: Yes it is. You don't care about her. You don't care about her baby. What you care about is what you think about yourself and how kind you are. But instead you, and people like you, make it necessary for the hospital to hire security like me, and spend time arguing with the public, like you, so any chance she might have to have a nice quiet single moment in hospital with her baby and her family is hijacked by public wellwishers and hangers-on.
ROSLYN [FIGURE 1]: Well. You seem to have found your voice.
SECURITY [FIGURE 3]: This is my voice and these is my words. Please leave and take your flowers with you.

>ROSLYN *exits. The* SECURITY GUARD *continues to stand.* RONALD [FIGURE 2] *enters.*

RONALD [FIGURE 2]: These are for Mrs Chamberlain.
SECURITY [FIGURE 3]: No.

>*1984.* LINDY *enters, in prison dress.*

LINDY: In April they revoked my bail and I was sent back in jail.

I got milk fever then because I had no baby to feed
no tablets
no nothing.
It all hurt
very badly.

She crosses her arms across her breasts.

And then I was returned to Darwin.

INMATE [FIGURE 1]: You're Lindy.

LINDY: Yes.

INMATE [FIGURE 1]: Chamberlain.

LINDY: Yes.

INMATE [FIGURE 1]: In here we don't talk about what you have or haven't done.

LINDY: Okay.

INMATE [FIGURE 1]: In here, you never question anyone.

LINDY: Sure.

INMATE [FIGURE 1]: You got the cell 'cross from solitary.

LINDY: Well, I'm just where they put me.

INMATE [FIGURE 1]: They're gonna bring Lily to solitary.

LINDY: Who's Lily?

INMATE [FIGURE 1]: You gonna look out for her?

LINDY: I don't know her.

INMATE [FIGURE 1]: Yeah. But you've got the cell 'cross from solitary. Just look out for her and tell us how she looks.

LINDY: When they open and shut the door?

INMATE [FIGURE 1]: You gonna hear her and you gonna smell her.

LINDY: Smell her?

INMATE [FIGURE 1]: There's a toilet in solitary, but Lily don't use it when she's going off.

Pause.

LINDY: Maybe we can ask to change cells?

INMATE [FIGURE 1]: I heard you were vegetarian.

LINDY: All my life.

INMATE [FIGURE 1]: The abattoir across the road. When they've been killing pigs all night. Now there's a smell for you. You lay awake, count the number of times the stun gun goes off. The pigs cry when they're being killed, the young pigs they sound like a baby screaming.

The INMATE *makes the sound of the stun gun going off. Over and over.*

LINDY: That's enough.

INMATE [FIGURE 1]: You'll keep an eye on Lily?

LINDY: Lily was from Alice Springs, but she elected to do her time in Darwin because there was one extra television channel in Darwin. Which, when I first heard that, it sounded … small … but after some time it turned out to be insightful. Lily was unstable. When I spoke to her in the afternoon she knew that she was unstable, she said, 'I'm going to do something soon, I'm going to get upset and I'm going to hurt someone'. She knew. And she used to pray, 'Please help me not to hurt someone and not to hurt myself'. I tried to calm her down. That was in the day. By that night she was screaming. When they tried to put her into a restraining belt she was struggling and swearing. I mean, she was using words that I had never even heard before.

Two male GUARDS [FIGURE 2 & FIGURE 3] *punch and subdue a struggling* LILY [FIGURE 1]. *Violently.*

They said she had once grabbed an officer and banged his head up and down on the concrete. They said she had once stabbed a screw [*guard*] with a kitchen knife when the screw was pregnant. They said a lot of things about Lily. And then when they transferred her, when they brought her out, her eyes were wild, her hair was matted with faeces, her clothes were dripping with urine and water from the handbasin.

GUARD [FIGURE 2]: Chamberlain, you've got a phone call.

LINDY: Me?

GUARD [FIGURE 2]: Yes, you.

LINDY: I knew it had to be bad because you weren't allowed calls. So I knew it had to be bad. My son, Reagan, had been standing watching a neighbour's bonfire when a glass bottle that had been thrown into the fire exploded. The shards of glass cut through the right side of his face, slicing his cornea and right eye.

REAGAN [FIGURE 3]: Mummy.

LINDY: He'd been asking for me since it happened.

REAGAN [FIGURE 3]: Mummy.

LINDY: And Reagan is not a child to ask. He's like me, he hides his

feelings, but he doesn't understand why he can't be comforted by his mother. They won't let me go down to Mulawa, they won't let me go down to see him, and if he comes to see me, the taking off and landing of getting on a plane is only going to put more pressure on his damaged eye.
REAGAN [FIGURE 3]: Mummy!
LINDY: That was … that was really hard. That was … I went down low that time. Lower than I'd been. Low. The next time the family came to visit, Reagan walked in the gate with an eye patch on, and then at the end of the visit when I went to say goodbye to him, he couldn't be found.
GUARD [FIGURE 1]: Reagan.
GUARD [FIGURE 2]: Reagan.

    LINDY *finds where* REAGAN *is hiding.*

LINDY: Reagan, you have to go home now, darling.
REAGAN [FIGURE 3]: Please let me stay here with you.
LINDY: I would love you to stay, darling, but I don't think they'll let you.
REAGAN [FIGURE 3]: I wouldn't be any trouble.
LINDY: I know you wouldn't, my little pirate.
REAGAN [FIGURE 3]: I can hide under the bed all day and then see you at night.
LINDY: At night we sleep with the lights on.

    A GUARD [FIGURE 1] *drags* REAGAN *out.*

REAGAN [FIGURE 3]: Please let me stay.
LINDY: I can't, Reagan. You have to go now.

    REAGAN *looks at her. Furious. Then runs off.*

It took me days to settle back into the prison routine. The routine I was now sentenced to, for life.

END OF ACT ONE

ACT TWO

The FIGURES *are a singing and dancing chorus.* LINDY *is still in her prison dress.*

KATH FISHER [FIGURE 1]: Dear Mrs Chamberlain, this is an official 'cheering up' type letter.
FIGURE 3: My washing isn't Omo bright
FIGURE 2: My kids won't stay asleep at night
FIGURE 3: I'm overweight
FIGURE 2: I hate my hair.
FIGURE 3: My dress is worn, no glamour there
FIGURE 2: The bills are always somehow paid
   But there's never any left … to … save.
ALL: [*singing*] I long to make my life complete
   My youth escapes on fleeting feet
   And though I love them earnestly
   I need a little time … for … me.
KATH FISHER [FIGURE 1]: Thought I'd write you a letter. Don't know why 'cause you'll probably not get to read it. I bet you get thousands. I wrote to you recently in response to an article I intend to give to an ex-step mummy. What? Oh, 'ex' step mummy because my dad and her got divorced when he became a lady.
FIGURE 3: The house is full of persistent dust
FIGURE 2: And creeping toys that feel they must
   Fill every room without a rest
FIGURE 3: I try I do I try my best
   But I never seem to get jobs done
   They keep on rising with … the … sun.
ALL: [*singing*] I long to make my life complete
   My youth escapes on fleeting feet
   And though I love them earnestly
   I need a little time … for … me.
KATH FISHER [FIGURE 1]: We've got jelly beans and Smarties in the

kitchen. When I walk in there they attack me and I must defend myself with my teeth. I went shopping for dresses last week. I usually fit into a sixteen or at least an eighteen, but I couldn't even fit into a twenty. How many fat ladies have you seen with wafer thin hips?

FIGURE 2: Three children battle night and day
   Demand attention right away
FIGURE 3: My friend had gained her B.S.C.
   But all I've got is M.A.D.
FIGURE 2: Hubby's in love with the TV set
   'Uh huh' and grunt is all ... I ... get.

ALL: [*singing*] I long to make my life complete
   My youth escapes on fleeting feet
   And though I love them earnestly
   I need a little time ... for ... me.

KATH FISHER [FIGURE 1]: Sincerely yours, Kath.
   I write poetry. Can't get it published though. I try.
   But as I write from the perspective of an outer Western suburban neurotic housewife suffering from severe melancholy and verging on insanity, I don't get many takers.

ALL: [*singing*] Whatever became of 'being in love'
   I guess the years gave that ... the ... shove.

   I long to make my life complete
   My youth escapes on fleeting feet
   And though I love them earnestly
   I need a little time for me
   I long to make my life complete
   My youth escapes on fleeting feet
   And though I love them earnestly
   I need a little time for me.

LINDY When I got this one I said to all the girls in jail, 'Look what I've got'. We laughed, because I loved the ones who wrote to cheer me up, not just tell me how they felt. I mean they meant well and all of them, everyone who wrote, that was lovely, but the ones I really cherished were the ones who didn't just want to tell me how much they pitied me or how sorry they felt for me. I mean think about it, being told you're a Christian martyr and pitiable, and tragic, doesn't exactly help you to get through the day! It's all very well to say that I'm like Paul and Daniel and Job, try being told that when you're trying to psych yourself up to get through another day in prison. Yeah, the letters I adored, and was really grateful for, were the ones that made me laugh.

ANONYMOUS [FIGURE 2]: What did the doorbell say to Lindy Chamberlain when she rang it?

Dingo dingo dingo.

ANONYMOUS [FIGURE 3]: What's a baby in a pram next to a dingo?

Meals on Wheels.

ANONYMOUS [FIGURE 1]: What do vegetarian dingoes eat?

Cabbage Patch kids.

What is the definition of revenge?

ANONYMOUS [FIGURE 2]: A baby with a dingo in its mouth.

ANONYMOUS [FIGURE 3]: What is the natural enemy of a test-tube baby?

Dingo with a straw.

LINDY: Did you hear the one about the Irish dingo?

He was found in the Darwin Botanical Gardens eating Azaleas.

SCENE: LEAFLETING THE MALL

MAVIS *is standing in the Darwin Mall, holding leaflets.* MIKE *passes her.*

MAVIS [FIGURE 1]: Can I give you one of these?

MIKE [FIGURE 3]: What is it, luv?

MAVIS [FIGURE 1]: It's a leaflet about how to help protest Lindy Chamberlain's innocence.

He stops stone still.

MIKE [FIGURE 3]: And why would I want to do that?

MAVIS [FIGURE 1]: Okay.

MIKE [FIGURE 3]: No, come on. Why?

MAVIS [FIGURE 1]: You clearly believe she's guilty.

MIKE [FIGURE 3]: Not me, luv, that'd be the courts, that'd be the judicial system.

MAVIS [FIGURE 1]: Well, I believe they've got it wrong.

MIKE [FIGURE 3]: Well, I don't believe a dingo can get a baby out of its jumpsuit by using scissors and then fold it up and leave it in a pile.

MAVIS [FIGURE 1]: Okay.

ACT TWO

MIKE [FIGURE 3]: Well, okay is not exactly an answer, luv.
MAVIS [FIGURE 1]: There are answers to what you're talking about but I'm not sure you want to be persuaded.
MIKE [FIGURE 3]: You calling me stupid?
MAVIS [FIGURE 1]: No.
MIKE [FIGURE 3]: Then if I'm not stupid I'm ignorant, am I?
MAVIS [FIGURE 1] Listen, if you don't want a leaflet don't worry about it.
MIKE [FIGURE 3]: Are you one of them?
MAVIS [FIGURE 1]: One of what?
MIKE [FIGURE 3]: One of that cult that she's part of?
MAVIS [FIGURE 1]: Seventh Day Adventists are not a cult.
MIKE [FIGURE 3]: God testing Abraham. A sacrifice in the wilderness. That's you lot, isn't it?
MAVIS [FIGURE 1]: Not literally. Not babies.
MIKE [FIGURE 3]: Not that you want to admit to.
MAVIS [FIGURE 1]: Sir, you are entitled to your opinion and I am entitled to mine.
MIKE [FIGURE 3]: Not when it involves cutting the throat of your children, you're not.

Pause.

MAVIS [FIGURE 1]: You know how I said I didn't think you were stupid, or ignorant. Well, I was mistaken.
MIKE [FIGURE 3]: You're saying that to me.
MAVIS [FIGURE 1]: Seems as if I am.
MIKE [FIGURE 3]: Not a very Christian attitude.
MAVIS [FIGURE 1]: Probably not. But you've got no right to speak to me like that either.
MIKE [FIGURE 3]: If you're gonna stand in a public mall and tell me a murdering bitch is innocent, I'd say I've got every right to say whatever I like to you.
MAVIS [FIGURE 1]: There's no need to get aggressive.
MIKE [FIGURE 3]: Women always say you're getting aggressive as soon as you disagree with them.
MAVIS [FIGURE 1]: There is no need to raise your voice.
MIKE [FIGURE 3]: I'm not raising my voice, I'm not being aggressive. I'm just speaking my mind. Which you invited me to do.

MAVIS [FIGURE 1]: You're scaring me.

MIKE [FIGURE 3]: And you're scaring me. With your blind ignorance and your misplaced loyalty.

MAVIS [FIGURE 1]: I'll call the police.

MIKE [FIGURE 3]: Fruit cake.

MAVIS [FIGURE 1]: Thug.

> MAVIS *withdraws to the other side of the stage.*

MIKE [FIGURE 3]: So how did the dingo get the baby out of the jumpsuit then? With no saliva on it.

> MAVIS *refuses to speak to him.*

It didn't, that's how. Because it was an adult fruit cake cult member who took the baby out and cut its throat, not a wild dog.

MAVIS [FIGURE 1]: Were you there, were you?

MIKE [FIGURE 3]: No, and neither were you.

MAVIS [FIGURE 1]: Yeah, but the person who was there says it was a dingo.

MIKE [FIGURE 3]: And hasn't she made that sound plausible.

MAVIS [FIGURE 1]: You're just an irrational bully.

MIKE [FIGURE 3]: And you're just an irrational believer.

MAVIS [FIGURE 1]: Get away from me.

MIKE [FIGURE 3]: Not all women love their children. Not all women accept their baby.

MAVIS [FIGURE 1]: Who didn't accept their baby?

MIKE [FIGURE 3]: First step is putting that murderer in jail, second step is shutting down the whole religious box and dice. Ban the bloody lot of you.

MAVIS [FIGURE 1]: Was it your wife?

MIKE [FIGURE 3]: I'll vote for that to happen. Now take your leaflets and stuff them up your backside.

> *He snatches the leaflets from her and throws them into the air.*

LINDY: You were only supposed to have two or three letters and one book in the cell at a time. So in the end it was, 'Here, Lindy, read 'em as quick as you can and get them back to us', and so I'd wait for the weekend and then just go through them. And after a while, when I was getting behind, the other girls in jail said, 'Can we help you?', and so once I'd read them and put them in one stack or the other they would take the names and addresses and list them up for answering. A lot of the letters had things in them, gifts and other things. Sometimes they might show me or I was told you've got such and such that's going in your property. It was just awkward when people sent me food. Perishable food. Which they did often in the beginning, and then I sent out the message, 'Please don't send food because we can't have it', but some people still would. The prison officers can't keep it because you might say they're stealing your food. And you're not allowed to have it so it can't be handed out. So I'd say, 'Can't we split it between everybody?' and they'd say, 'No, it's not allowed because it might have drugs injected into it so it just has to go in the bin'.

JENNY [FIGURE 1]: Dear Lindy,

I spoke to Pastor Douglas Weir about writing to you and he gave me an address to where I could write. I would very much like to be a friend so if you like to answer you are only too welcome. Lindy please don't give up your trust in our Lord Jesus. He is the only one who can help us in our hours of need. You know when my husband starts getting into me, I always say a little piece I got from a book I once read. May be you already heard it before and I think it is beautiful when I am hurting.

    He's able. He's able
    I know He is able.
    I know my Lord is able
    to carry me through.
    He heals the broken-hearted
    He sets the captive free.
    He brings the dead to life again
    and calms the troubled sea.

Well Lindy you are in my prayers I really do hope you would like to write. You know all my friends are by mail you know they are very rewarding.

From a friend,

Jenny.

P.S. I use the post office as my husband doesn't believe in me having friends.

GLENDON [FIGURE 2]: My dear Lindy,
I'd like to tell you a little coincidence.

As I knelt to pray near my bed I looked out at the skies and shadowed by the mid-night moon, a huge Flindersia tree about fifty feet high was outlined against the soft light. It showed the upper half as a distinct profile of a human face with all the features clearly outlined and suddenly I saw the strong likeness—it was 'Lindy Chamberlain'—and so distinctly. There was a very slight breeze as if it were speaking and the eyes blinking occasionally. It is still there and others also see it. So until the tree changes its foliage we have that profile against the sky.

SCENE: THE SCHOOLYARD

GREG [FIGURE 1]: Hey, Reagan. Your mum killed your baby, dropkick.
REAGAN [FIGURE 3]: Did not.
GREG [FIGURE 1]: Did so.
REAGAN [FIGURE 3]: Did not.
GREG [FIGURE 1]: Court says she did.
REAGAN [FIGURE 3]: Yeah, well the court is wrong.
GREG [FIGURE 1]: Chances.
REAGAN [FIGURE 3]: A dingo took the baby. I remember it stepping on my back.
GREG [FIGURE 1]: Then why didn't you stop it?
REAGAN [FIGURE 3]: Because I was sleeping.
GREG [FIGURE 1]: Then how can you remember that it stepped on you?
REAGAN [FIGURE 3]: It woke me up.
GREG [FIGURE 1]: That's what your mum does, right? Changes her story.
REAGAN [FIGURE 3]: You know nothing.
GREG [FIGURE 1]: You know what, that's true. But the courts know things and they don't say people do things if they don't.
REAGAN [FIGURE 3]: They do. All the time.
GREG [FIGURE 1]: Why would they?
REAGAN [FIGURE 3]: How should I know?
GREG [FIGURE 1]: That's because they wouldn't.
REAGAN [FIGURE 3]: I'm not talking to you.
GREG [FIGURE 1]: Good. Then I'll just stare at you.

GREG *stares at* REAGAN.

REAGAN [FIGURE 3]: Go away.
GREG [FIGURE 1]: You go.
REAGAN [FIGURE 3]: I was here first.
GREG [FIGURE 1]: I was here second.
REAGAN [FIGURE 3]: Just go away. Just go away, you little shit.
GREG [FIGURE 1]: If your mum hears you saying shit you'll be fucked.
REAGAN [FIGURE 3]: Yeah, what's she gonna do?
GREG [FIGURE 1]: Wash your mouth out with laundry soap again.
REAGAN [FIGURE 3]: She can't do anything to me now. She can't even make me tidy my room.
GREG [FIGURE 1]: I wish they'd send my mum to jail.
REAGAN [FIGURE 3]: No you don't.
GREG [FIGURE 1]: If they did, I wouldn't just sit around doing nothing. I'd become Spider-Man and break her out. I'd turn into a superhero and cut through the bars with my laser vision.
REAGAN [FIGURE 3]: There is no such thing as a superhero. There's not even any adults that can help. All that kid's stuff is a lie. Why don't you just grow up?

> REAGAN *goes over to* GREG, *raising his fist in threat. A moment, then he lowers his fist. He sits onstage, a forlorn figure.*

LINDY: Reagan got into hardly any fights. Well, apparently he got into one pretty early on. He was drinking at a bubbler and this other kid tried to push him into the bubbler and then when he couldn't he tried to punch Reagan. Reagan suddenly dodged and moved aside so the kid's punch landed on the wall and he broke his hand. And from then on people assumed Reagan broke this kid's hand and left him alone. But Aidan apparently got into a lot of fights.
AIDAN [FIGURE 2]: 5 December 1985.
Avondale College, Cooranbong.
Dear Mr Tuxworth and Mr Hawke,
I cannot understand why you are keeping my Mummy in jail when I know she did not kill my baby sister Azaria.
My mummy loved bubby just as we all did and I was with Mummy and talking to her the hole [sic] time. I miss my Mum and Kahlia and Reagan and Dad do to [sic].

Is there nothing you can do to help me?
Yours sincerely,
Aidan Chamberlain

REAGAN [FIGURE 3]: 5th December 1985.
Avondale College, Cooranbong.
Dear Mr Tuxworth, Mr Hawke, Prince Charles and Princess Diana,
I can still remember the dingo walking on my chest.
I loved my bubby Azaria and so did Mommy
We need Mummy at home so does Kahlia need a mommy
Can you make them let my mum come home to me
From Reagan.

During the following speech LINDY *physically becomes smaller and more broken.*

GORDON [FIGURE 1]: Dear Lindy,
I think that this must be the hardest letter I have had to write to you yet. Words cannot express the feelings of frustration and annoyance we feel. It is just so unfair. You poor people have become public property for all to speculate about, and to judge and condemn. It is not often that sleep evades me but last week when Channel Ten screened its reconstruction of events in its two-hour film, I couldn't sleep a wink. Sally cried through most of it, and likewise couldn't sleep. Why do people believe only what they want to believe? If things were different, you wouldn't be where you are now. The ignorant, foolish and stupid comments that people make causes me to wonder. On the other hand the foolish are tempered by the thinking, sensitive people in our society. Thank goodness they are there. I was just thinking the other night, after I had attended the rally in the Town Hall, that the Lord hasn't deserted you (I know that you are well aware of that) but how remarkable that the principal witnesses of that fatal night—namely the Wests and the Lowes—and the subsequent trial witnesses—Les Harris and Professor Boetcher—are people of such integrity, conviction and action. They all feel so strongly about the miscarriage of justice that they are prepared to travel around Australia speaking to large crowds and influential people, to clear your name? What if the witnesses were more expedient people who couldn't have cared less about you after the trial? It is at a great price I know, but hang in there

ACT TWO 35

Lindy. The battle is by no means over. Thousands of people are determined to see you released. Your case will not settle down. Many wish it would blow away and be forgotten, but it will not. The issues are too great to ignore and the future integrity of our legal system hangs upon resolving the issue. I just wish I could do something more to comfort you and Mike. It is so fascinating. I will share this with you: I was talking to Les Harris on Friday night, and he said something I thought was beautiful. He said something to this effect, 'I would like to go up to Berrimah Goal and talk with Lindy and if I could, I would take her hands in mine and tell her "Sweetie, I know you are innocent and I am going to do all I can to get you out of here".'
Gordon.

During the next speech LINDY *gathers her courage, vocally and physically.*

LINDY: [*quoting from her own letters*] 'For over five years now I have lived with rumours, innuendo and accusations over the death of my baby daughter, Azaria. I have tried to co-operate in all ways possible, but still this farce continues. For nearly three years I have worked as an inmate of this prison for the NT Government for thirty cents per day trying to do whatever I was asked pleasantly and politely whether I liked it or not, without causing trouble. I have used available legal means and sought an inquiry whereby the NT Government had a chance to redeem their own name. In return they have ignored decency and justice and still scoff at it.

'As an innocent person who has gone the second mile and turned the other cheek, I will no longer stand quietly by and serve a corrupt system. As from one p.m., Darwin time today (Friday 1st November '85), I am refusing to work in any way whatsoever for this prison and the government it represents.

'I did not kill my beloved daughter and I refuse to be treated as a criminal any longer.'

I had already smuggled a duplicate of the letter out for a press release. I was going to walk in and hand it to the guards, and the same time Senator Bob Collins was going to read it out at a press conference in Darwin. That way they couldn't deny I had given it to them. But I had to postpone it because Michael wanted to visit with the kids and if I gave the letter to the guards they wouldn't have let me see the kids, I would have been put in lockdown with no visitors. I only just managed to stop it in time. And then everything changed.

FIGURE 1: [*whispering*] Something's been found at the Rock

FIGURE 2: Prepare yourself for a shock

FIGURE 3: It's part of a baby-sized frock.

LINDY: Like most things in this case I saw it on the news, this time on the television in the prison common area.

FIGURE 1: A body's been found in that hell

FIGURE 2: A tourist went missing and fell

FIGURE 3: And nearby this jacket as well.

> *They pass the dirt-stained jacket from one to the other, finally passing it to* LINDY *who looks at it, wordlessly.*

FIGURE 1: A white, knitted, stained matinee

FIGURE 2: It's just like you always did say

FIGURE 3: It's the one she was wearing that day?

> LINDY *nods.*

FIGURE 1: With pale lemon edging around

FIGURE 2: The testified piece has been found

FIGURE 3: Release will be made on those grounds.

> *Onstage, the* FIGURES *remove* LINDY's *prison outfit and dress, revealing her release suit underneath.*
>
> *1986.*

SUSAN GLASSON [FIGURE 1]: Ansett Flight 1043, Darwin to Sydney, 9th February, 1986.

Dear Lindy,

On behalf of the flight attendants, we'd really like to wish every success in all you do in the coming years, and naturally peace and happiness with your loved ones and family. You are a truly marvellous lady.

Susan Glasson and crew.

FIGURE 2: Steve and Judy wrote a fax.

FIGURE 3: Free.

FIGURE 2: A single, one-word fax.

FIGURE 1: 'Free'.

FIGURE 3: Oh joy, oh joy, oh joy, oh joy.
FIGURE 2: You're free!

The FIGURES *throw yellow ribbons into the air.*

FIGURE 1: To be, to be, to be.
FIGURE 3: You're free.
FIGURE 1: You're free.
FIGURE 2: You're free.
FIGURE 3: In blue texta calligraphy.
FIGURE 1: There's just no better single word.
FIGURE 2: Free.
FIGURE 1: You're home and hosed and back on track
FIGURE 3: Free.
FIGURE 2: You're out and gone and done and free.
FIGURE 1: Lindy, you are really free!
FIGURE 3: Glee and giggle, tea and twee
FIGURE 1: Buzzy banshee burgundy
FIGURE 2: I'm jumping like a jumping flea.
FIGURE 3: You're free, you're free, you're free, you're free.
 All Steve and Judy and the fax said, 'FREE'!
LINDY: As soon as he'd heard I'd been released, this lovely man, Ian, tied yellow ribbons all down the drive on the road home, all on the gate and on the trees. It was just like the song.

Pause.

ANONYMOUS [FIGURE 1]: [*singing*] Once a jolly pastor
 Camped in a caravan
 Under the shade of a kurrajong tree,
 And he sang and he prayed
 As he watched the baby's bottle boil,
 'You'll be a Seventh Day Adventist like me'.

ANONYMOUS [FIGURE 3]: If you think that it was the end of a nightmare, we've got news for you. Your guilty conscience is only just starting to haunt you. You may have two hundred and fifty friends to celebrate with, but you have millions of people whom you still have to convince about your innocence, which you'll never be able to do.
 Have you ever looked around when you go shopping, how people watch you with sneering glances. One day it'll be all in the

news again, and someone will find the remains of your murdered baby girl.

ANONYMOUS [FIGURE 1]: [*singing*] Down came Lindy to snatch up Azaria,
>She picked up the scissors and stabbed her with glee
And she smiled as she shoved
That baby in the camera bag.
'It's fun being a Seventh Day Adventist like me.'

>Out came a dingo, nosing round the camp fire
Lindy winked at Michael and said 'It wasn't me'
What happened to the baby you put in the camera bag?
Give it to the dingo and you'll get off scot free.

>Give it to the dingo,
Give it to the dingo,
Give it to the dingo,
And you'll get off scot free.

>Up jumped the dingo and ran past the camera bag
'You'll never blame Azaria's murder on me'
And her ghost may be heard as you pass
By the kurrajong,
'Mummy was the one who did away with me'.

May you fry in Hell, you bitch.

LINDY: If people think they're not safe and there's nothing to protect them, including the law, they panic. And so they think that the system is basically fair but made a mistake in my case. That's not true. And I have to face, and my children growing up had to face, that everything that you're encouraged to believe in as a child is not true. It can make you streetwise but it can also make you insecure and it can make you suspicious and a bit paranoid maybe, but the other word is that you can become … cynical. You can start questioning everybody and trust is difficult. But you can't live without trust.

Each time someone betrays you, you tend to die a little inside, which means to an onlooker that you seem to handle it better. You don't, you just learn to deal with the pain. So anyone looking on thinks, 'Oh well, she took that well'. You've coped with it before so you will get through it again. You will be okay. It doesn't hurt any less. But you can't live without pain.

ACT TWO

MALCOLM BROWN [FIGURE 2]: Ermington, New South Wales.
18 November, 1990.
Dear Lindy,
I have written to Avis and Cliff, Ivan and Greta and to Michael, following my series of articles on the end of your marriage. I sought not to shed crocodile tears or to justify myself and I won't to you. As I walked out, I said to the Editor who had requested the story, 'I've just dynamited ten years of relationships'.

Peter Bowers, a veteran *Herald* journalist, consoled me last Friday. He said it was the hardest thing to do, to break a story adverse to people whom you had grown to like and respect, and had some measure of trust in you. On the one hand, as a journalist you are required to get close to people. On the other, when the story breaks, you are expected to use the intimate knowledge you have of them to produce better reports than your opposition.

If I had any control of the story (i.e. if it was between you and me and Michael), I might have been able to hold it for the time you requested. But after Col Allison (doing his duty) had told the *Herald* editorship what was happening, and after it became clear the story had gone beyond Cooranbong, I had no real option but to break it. It gave me no pleasure, especially in view of the suffering of the entire family, and after the nice things you had said about me.

Even though I remain a journalist and not a public relations man, and have my first loyalty to my employer, I am still prepared to pledge the services available through me to do whatever I can for the welfare of you, of Michael, and of your three beautiful and long-suffering children.
Malcolm Brown.

LINDY: His twin brother committed suicide and he wrote all about it and there was a big estrangement in the family for a long time, you know, how dare he expose the dirty linen, but that was his way of coping. And he met his wife through a dating service. He was asked to do a piece on dating services and he said, 'Oh well, put me down', and he met her through that and got kids and all of that. And he kept in touch with my mum forever. He's an odd fellow, but I like him anyway. When my verdict of 'guilty' was announced he was the first one to leap to his feet, shake his fists and yell out, 'Bastards'.

GAYLE HANNAH [FIGURE 1]: Kuranda, Far North Queensland.
26 February, 1991.
Dear Lindy,
Over ten years ago a ten and a half foot Amethystine python tried to take my not quite two year old son from his bed. He doesn't really remember it and it has passed into family mythology by now. However, this weekend I attended a writer's workshop with the wonderful writer/poet Kate Llewellyn and after reading the enclosed poem she said I MUST send it to you and so here it is. I hope it says something to you. I feel that in your case the mystery is deep and light may never reach all the corners but Life is larger and deeper and higher and wider than most of us are brave enough to admit.
With love,
Gayle.

> The Letter I should Have Written to Lindy Chamberlain
>
> I believe you, Lindy,
> I know that even now with all that is tamed
> the Wild is always near
> In the black of night
> I lifted my child from his winter bed
> only to feel a cold weight, skin to skin
> along my length.
> Python jaws around my baby's leg.
> Two days later on TV,
> whodunit: the Dingo or the Bitch
> But I believed you and I wonder
> Would they have hissed at me on the steamy courthouse steps:
> 'The snake is innocent.'

LINDY: If you've got to be on your best behaviour all the time, out in public, that's wearing. More and more I've been thinking lately … 'What's it matter?' Every now and then I'll do something and I'll think, 'Oh, did anyone see me do that?' And I'm like, 'I'm too old to care'. And I might as well be myself because somebody is sure to condemn me, either way.

ANONYMOUS [FIGURE 3]: Jan 22nd, 1991.
Dear Lindy,
Some months ago the Lord told me that you were innocent, that a dog

really did take your baby. Up until this time I felt you were guilty as many did and I was terribly wrong. And I would like to say to you how very sorry I feel for thinking that and ask your forgiveness.

Today, Lindy, the Lord told me why your baby was taken. I have no idea if you know, but unmistakably, the Lord our God has shown me why you have suffered so much and it is to draw the attention of the whole world to the place where it happened. For in the immediate future there will begin a fantastic spiritual event, and this gospel revival will come out of Brisbane this year and will be the event that looks to the gathering of the elect of God, the Church of the Firstborn, as prophesied since old testament times. This gathering will be an incredible work of the Lord, a marvellous work and a wonder and he will do a strange thing—as Jeremiah prophesied, a new thing he will do in the Earth and it will be initiated and guided by women. This gathering will continue throughout 1991 ready for the return of the Saviour to the Earth in 1992 to collect the Pure in Heart—his people—and this gathering will culminate at Ayers Rock.

And the Lord has told me that you have played your part so well in bringing the attention of the World to the gathering place. Because of your suffering, Lindy, the Whole World knows of Ayers Rock, Central Australia where the gathering will culminate and all of God's people, Zion, will be removed from the Earth in preparation for the wicked to be burned.

LINDY *sits centre stage, surrounded by boxes.*

NEIL [FIGURE 2]: Gwynedd, North Wales, Great Britain.
HELEN [FIGURE 3]: North Croydon.
BARBARA [FIGURE 1]: Collingwood, Victoria.
ALL: Dear Lindy, Dear Lindy, Dear Mrs Chamberlain.
NEIL [FIGURE 2]: Where does one start?
HELEN [FIGURE 3]: Lindy I am going to be very honest with you, so please, I don't mean to hurt you.
BARBARA [FIGURE 1]: Please excuse the self-indulgent nature of this letter. I know, in part, I am relieving a guilty conscience.
HELEN [FIGURE 3]: I thought you were guilty of killing Azaria. One day I was walking past a bookshop and there was your book *Through My Eyes*.

ALL: *Through my Eyes*.

HELEN [FIGURE 3]: I couldn't afford to buy it, but I couldn't put it back, the next thing I knew I was walking out with it.

NEIL [FIGURE 2]: It is the best book that I have ever read and am ever likely to read, because it is the first book that has ever made me cry, I'm not ashamed to admit it, not many eighteen-year-old boys will take the chance to read your book and even fewer will admit to crying at every piece of bad luck or misfortune that you suffered.

BARBARA [FIGURE 1]: It was 2 a.m. this morning when I finished your book and first wrote this letter. So moved was I that I wanted to write straight away.

HELEN [FIGURE 3]: I had read four pages and I had started to cry.

NEIL [FIGURE 2]: How could the justice system have allowed such an injustice to go unheeded for so long? How could it ever have been allowed to start? It is beyond comprehension.

BARBARA [FIGURE 1]: I look from the cover photo to those of you in custody to those of you after your release and I am so sad, so amazed and so angry.

HELEN [FIGURE 3]: I knew I had branded you a killer and the only criminal here was me.

NEIL [FIGURE 2]: I want to say how sorry I am, but then I don't suppose you want people to feel pity for you. I always thought that Britain had some terrible press but Australia seems to be streaking ahead.

BARBARA [FIGURE 1]: I was wrong. I am very sorry for any hurt I may have inflicted upon you and your family. I am ashamed that I have never done anything to help you. I am so sorry you lost your baby daughter. I am so sorry your country delighted in your suffering. You were the victim of a witch-hunt.

HELEN [FIGURE 3]: I'm sorry Australia is losing you, but perhaps we don't deserve you.

NEIL [FIGURE 2]: I marvel at your ability to cope. I am not especially religious, I am a believer and your book has helped me to place trust in God.

BARBARA [FIGURE 1]: The last chapter of the book is so powerful and moving. You cut right through the crap and slapped me in the face, saying 'How dare you judge me so unfairly?!'

HELEN [FIGURE 3]: I have read the *Women's Day* article about your future husband. Congratulations to you and Rick. I looked at the photos and I could see the love in your eyes (Rick also).

You are right, you belong to each other.

NEIL [FIGURE 2]: With love and best wishes,
Neil.

BARBARA [FIGURE 1]: Sincerely,
Barbara.

HELEN [FIGURE 3]: There is so much too I would like to still say but I feel if I get started I won't be able to stop.

All the best for your future Lindy ...

Yours,

Helen.

LINDY: There's one letter that is really significant to me and I really relate to it.

Long pause, she is tearful.

My parents took an interest in this young man who came out from England and my parents kind of adopted him and he lived at our place for twelve months or more and I think they sponsored him. Mum did a bit of matchmaking and Dad ended up marrying him to his wife and then ... their little boy was pageboy for Michael and I at our wedding and he sort of calls himself my other big brother and he sent this card ...

She is crying.

Actually a friend's mum died and I thought of it last night. All it said in there was 'My heart bleeds', and, I thought, that says more than anything I have had said to me. You know there's a lot of platitudes. Believe me, we got them all. And you can tell when it's just 'This is what I think I should say' or it's 'Something has happened to me and I mean this to you'. It was just so pithy. And he was never a touchy feely sort of a guy. So it was really lovely to get it because I'd been out of touch maybe five or six years. Then just out of the blue get this ... and I thought ... oh, wow. Presumably that's in with what Michael's got but it's not hard to remember it. My heart bleeds, Alan.

LINDY *exits.*

THE LIBRARIANS

LIBRARIAN [FIGURE 2]: So did you actually meet her? When we were acquiring her papers for the library? Lindy I mean?

LIBRARIAN [FIGURE 3]: Yeah, I've met her a couple of times now.

LIBRARIAN [FIGURE 2]: So what's she like?

LIBRARIAN [FIGURE 3]: She's … really funny.

LIBRARIAN [FIGURE 2]: Funny strange?

LIBRARIAN [FIGURE 3]: No, she's got a great sense of humour. Puts you at ease very quickly.

LIBRARIAN [FIGURE 2]: She'd have had a lot of practice at that, I suppose.

LIBRARIAN [FIGURE 3]: She told me this great story about her and Meryl going out to a mall, some mall, shopping for clothes when they were making the film, and no-one recognised Meryl Streep and everyone mobbed Lindy.

LIBRARIAN [FIGURE 2]: Well, she's obviously very conscious of her fame.

LIBRARIAN [FIGURE 3]: Why do you say that?

LIBRARIAN [FIGURE 2]: Because she must be.

LIBRARIAN [FIGURE 3]: I don't think she asked to be famous.

LIBRARIAN [FIGURE 2]: I'm just saying she's never shied away from the media.

LIBRARIAN [FIGURE 3]: You thought she was guilty?

LIBRARIAN [FIGURE 2]: How is that relevant?

LIBRARIAN [FIGURE 3]: Did you?

LIBRARIAN [FIGURE 2]: I didn't really have an opinion.

LIBRARIAN [FIGURE 3]: No-one didn't have an opinion.

LIBRARIAN [FIGURE 2]: Well, I didn't.

LIBRARIAN [FIGURE 3]: There are three things that have divided this nation right down the centre. Conscription, Whitlam and Lindy Chamberlain.

Pause.

LIBRARIAN [FIGURE 2]: Alright, I thought she was guilty.

LIBRARIAN [FIGURE 3]: Seriously?

LIBRARIAN [FIGURE 2]: I still think she's guilty.

LIBRARIAN [FIGURE 3]: How can you?

LIBRARIAN [FIGURE 2]: My whole family thought she was guilty. It would be a betrayal of family tradition to change my mind.

ACT TWO

LIBRARIAN [FIGURE 3]: You're joking.
LIBRARIAN [FIGURE 2]: Sort of.
LIBRARIAN [FIGURE 3]: But not really.
LIBRARIAN [FIGURE 2]: No. Not really.
LIBRARIAN [FIGURE 3]: But that's crazy.
LIBRARIAN [FIGURE 2]: In your opinion.
LIBRARIAN [FIGURE 3]: Not in my opinion. In truth.
LIBRARIAN [FIGURE 2]: We'll just have to agree to disagree.
LIBRARIAN [FIGURE 3]: No we won't, because she's not guilty.
LIBRARIAN [FIGURE 2]: I am entitled to my opinion.
LIBRARIAN [FIGURE 3]: But it's not an opinion. It's a lie.
LIBRARIAN [FIGURE 2]: I'm not going to change my mind.
LIBRARIAN [FIGURE 3]: But why not?
LIBRARIAN [FIGURE 2]: Because I don't want to.

Pause.

LIBRARIAN [FIGURE 3]: You're intelligent enough to know that that's madness.
LIBRARIAN [FIGURE 2]: You asked me to be honest. And then you don't like what I honestly think. How old were you when it happened … Seven? Nine? I was thirty and I remember it, vividly. She was cold and unfeeling. I wasn't convinced by her story and I wasn't the only one … our whole town was pretty much unanimous in thinking she did it.
LIBRARIAN [FIGURE 3]: Perhaps something here will change your mind.
LIBRARIAN [FIGURE 2]: There's nothing that exceptional about the letters themselves. I mean, a lot of them, many of them, are badly written.
LIBRARIAN [FIGURE 3]: [*passionately*] It's not about how they're written.
LIBRARIAN [FIGURE 2]: Then why bother keeping them?
LIBRARIAN [FIGURE 3]: Every scrap of paper, every instance of memory, has its place. Cold? This collection is testament to one of the most devoted mothers in the history of Australia. Unfeeling? Because she didn't perform the waterworks of hysterical grief for six months and then move on? She has taken every piece of paper associated with Azaria and every emotion that she has inspired and filed it like the most precious works of scholarship. This mother is still cherishing this baby and she will go on cherishing her and enshrining her 'til

her own death. Don't you get it?

This a memorial for Azaria Chamberlain.

2016. LINDY *enters, in contemporary dress.*

LINDY: I had this experience and it happened to me when I was in my early twenties. It was one of the first baptisms Michael ever did and I was sitting there and enjoying it. Being baptised was this girl, I don't know if there was a guy as well, but I remember her, and I remember thinking I cannot believe she is so young, she was gorgeous. She had an eighteen-month-old baby and she was seventeen and a half and married, he was twenty-six or something or other. During the service, I saw her looking at me a number of times and I saw her go like that [*Makes a flicking, fly-away action*] and I thought, what a funny thing. She did it two or three times and I wondered what was going on.

They'd invited us over for lunch. And so we went to lunch and I think we were setting the table or something and she said to me, 'Why did you do that?' and I said, 'What?' and she said, 'All those angels to blind me' and I was like, 'What!' and she said, 'Those angels around you, didn't you see them?' and I said, 'No, I didn't have anybody with me' and she said, 'Yes, you did. They were all around you and they were so bright I couldn't look at you.' And she said to me, 'Wow, if you've got that many angels you really must have something special to do' and I'm thinking, 'Yeah, okay, I know you're a new Christian and you're pretty keen. This is probably taking things a little too far, but I'm not going to burst your bubble now and anyway, who am I to judge?'

But then, I can tell you when I was in prison I often used to think, 'Maybe she really did see angels'. Just because I couldn't see them doesn't mean that she couldn't. And you may judge me for this too, but anyway, here goes. Sometimes I think they were all my angels.

Slowly gently, one by one, letters detach themselves from the piles and flutter up into the air.

Then hundreds of large white feathers float down to the stage.

The FIGURES *hum a lullaby under the following.*

ACT TWO

ELIZABETH MORRIS [FIGURE 1]: Dated this day 12th June, 2012.
I find that the name of the deceased was Azaria Chantel Loren Chamberlain, born in Mount Isa, Queensland, on 11 June 1980. I find that she was the daughter of Michael Leigh Chamberlain and Alice Lynne Chamberlain. I find that she died at Uluru, then known as Ayers Rock, on 17 August 1980. I find that the cause of her death was the result of being attacked and taken by a dingo.
Elizabeth Morris.
Coroner.

GLORIA KIMBER [FIGURE 2]: Stirling, South Australia.
Dear Lindy Chamberlain-Creighton,
I met you once in Miller Anderson's in Adelaide when you were autographing your book *Through My Eyes*. 'To the Kimbers,' you wrote in mine, and then added 'God Bless'.

I went away with a lump in my throat. Despite all you had suffered in prison and through cruel court decisions you could still find compassion in your heart to bless complete strangers, I hope you have found happiness in your life away from Australia, but I am glad you have come home. I wish you and yours contentment in the future.
Sincerely,
Gloria Kimber (Childs)

LINDY: Lullaby (For Azaria)
  by Gloria Kimber
  [*Singing*]
    O sing the child to sleep now,
    And sanctify the hours;
    In a contrite coming touch her,
    And cover her with flowers.

    O sing the child to sleep now,
    The beautiful—the blest—
    'Tis the time to hush the voices,
    To let the baby rest.

    O sing the child to sleep now,
    And weep a well of tears
    For a mother's lonely anguish—
    The torment of her years.

O sing the child to sleep now,
In recompense for wrong,
Tho' the melody is haunting,
And bitter-sweet the song.

THE END

Lindy Chamberlain-Creighton and Alana Valentine at the opening of Letters to Lindy *at the Canberra Theatre Centre.*

www.currency.com.au

Visit Currency Press' website now to:
- Buy your books online
- Browse through our full list of titles, from plays to screenplays, books on theatre, film and music, and more
- Choose a play for your school or amateur performance group by cast size and gender
- Obtain information about performance rights
- Find out about theatre productions and other performing arts news across Australia
- For students, read our study guides
- For teachers, access syllabus and other relevant information
- Sign up for our email newsletter

The performing arts publisher